Microeconomics

Political Economy and Development

Published in association with the
International Initiative for Promoting Political Economy (IIPPE)

Edited by
Ben Fine (SOAS, University of London)
Dimitris Milonakis (University of Crete)

Political economy and the theory of economic and social development have long been fellow travellers, sharing an interdisciplinary and multidimensional character. Over the last 50 years, mainstream economics has become totally formalistic, attaching itself to increasingly narrow methods and techniques at the expense of other approaches. Despite this narrowness, neoclassical economics has expanded its domain of application to other social sciences, but has shown itself incapable of addressing social phenomena and coming to terms with current developments in the world economy.

With world financial crises no longer a distant memory, and neoliberal scholarship and postmodernism in retreat, prospects for political economy have strengthened. It allows constructive liaison between the dismal and other social sciences and rich potential in charting and explaining combined and uneven development.

The objective of this series is to support the revival and renewal of political economy, both in itself and in dialogue with other social sciences. Drawing on rich traditions, we invite contributions that constructively engage with heterodox economics, critically assess mainstream economics, address contemporary developments and offer alternative policy prescriptions.

Also available

Theories of Social Capital:
Researchers Behaving Badly
Ben Fine

The Political Economy of Development:
The World Bank, Neoliberalism and Development Research
Edited by Kate Bayliss, Ben Fine and Elisa Van Waeyenberge

Dot.compradors:
Crisis and Corruption in the Indian Software Industry
Jyoti Saraswati

Beyond the Developmental State:
Industrial Policy into the Twenty-First Century
Edited by Ben Fine, Jyoti Saraswati and Daniela Tavasci

Macroeconomics:
A Critical Companion
Ben Fine and Ourania Dimakou

Microeconomics
A Critical Companion

Ben Fine

PlutoPress
www.plutobooks.com

First published 2016 by Pluto Press
345 Archway Road, London N6 5AA

www.plutobooks.com

British Library Cataloguing in Publication Data
A catalogue record for this book is available from the British Library

ISBN   978 0 7453 3602 2   Hardback
ISBN   978 0 7453 3607 7   Paperback
ISBN   978 1 7837 1779 8   PDF eBook
ISBN   978 1 7837 1781 1   Kindle eBook
ISBN   978 1 7837 1780 4   EPUB eBook

This book is printed on paper suitable for recycling and made from fully managed
and sustained forest sources. Logging, pulping and manufacturing processes are
expected to conform to the environmental standards of the country of origin.

Typeset by Stanford DTP Services, Northampton, England

Simultaneously printed in the European Union and United States of America

Contents

List of Boxes

List of Diagrams

Preface, Preliminaries and Acknowledgements

Having taught microeconomics at graduate level under various guises for more than 40 years, I have finally succumbed to the temptation to put on paper some of the content of what I have taught. This book represents the results for the microeconomics, and the counterpart volume, *Macroeconomics: A Critical Companion*, is published simultaneously. As with the lectures themselves, this has presented a number of difficulties. First, students and potential readers arrive with very different backgrounds. Most might have an undergraduate degree in economics and have covered the elementary principles of the mainstream and more. If so, and if they have retained that knowledge, some of what follows might be thought of as unnecessary. Nonetheless, it is almost inevitable that reviewing such material is more than worthwhile in light of doing so from a critical perspective. It is always handy to target material over which, from my own experience as teacher, students tend to stumble either in attempting to understand what is going on or in moving from one step to the next in algebraic derivation. To this end, I have provided a number of boxes dedicated to particular topics to supplement the text. Some are technical, some are not, but the material is hopefully laid out in a way that is clear and easy to follow. Second, for many students microeconomics is technically demanding in terms of mathematical requirements. So, it is necessary to deploy and command technical material, both as skill acquisition in and of itself and to gain a sense of the nature of microeconomics on the technical terms on which it is so dependent. As a result, many microeconomics textbooks are disproportionately mathematical in content, difficult to follow, and negligent of the motivation for, and significance of, one damn model after another. The difficulty here is to offer some select technical material without it becoming a goal in its own right, at the expense of the substantive content.

Third, microeconomics now covers a vast and growing weight of subject matter, both within and between topics. As with technical material, a judicious choice has to be made across the breadth and depth of material presented.

Fourth, unlike most other texts on microeconomics, the critical stance adopted here leaves open the option of presenting some alternatives to the mainstream. Again, this is done selectively for illustrative purposes but without pursuing issues too far, although some further issues and readings are raised at the end of each chapter (apart from some indulgent referencing of my own work, the presumption is that, given the capacity of the Internet, it is both desirable and possible for students to find further readings for themselves of the sort that best match their interests and capabilities). In short, the goal is to introduce students to alternative ways of thinking, often ways that were the orthodoxy but have now been discouraged and excluded from students' previous training, often rendering the idea of alternatives and alternative thinking both counter-intuitive and subject to resistance if not incomprehension. This too is uneven across the chapters, with greater or lesser emphasis on the mainstream, the technical material, the critique and alternatives.

Fifth, this is to compensate for the unavoidable fact that the vast majority of economics students, even those entering postgraduate study, are dismally unaware of methodological issues, of the history of their own discipline, of knowledge of alternatives to the mainstream, and of longstanding criticisms of the mainstream which are rarely acknowledged let alone countered. This adds to the weight of material that might be covered as well the difficulties of com-municating it and its importance.

Last, one of the problems in teaching economics in general, and micro-economics in particular, is that the technical demands can be so heavy upon students that they take up an undue weight of care and attention, in disproportion to the significance of what is being communicated. It takes a moment to say that maybe utility maximisation is neither the only motivation of consumers nor the best way to look at consumption, but it takes much longer and is more demanding to explain that the existence of utility functions depend upon a set of axioms – that preferences are binary, reflexive, transitive, complete and continuous (something not covered in this text). But which of these is the more important? Of course, ease of expression and learning is far from the only or main criteria of what it is important to cover and how, but there are clearly some trade-offs, to employ the vernacular, to make. I am endlessly surprised how students of economics are accomplished in the techniques they have been taught without simultaneously having developed conceptual understandings and a keen sense of what is important, in terms of both what is within the material and what is not.

Over the years, I hope to have found ways of addressing, if not overcoming, these difficulties of what to teach and how through including topics, and ways of presenting them, that compromise across the various demands and obstacles detailed above. In addition, during my time at SOAS over the past 20 years or more, given its additional preoccupation with issues related to development, there has been even less teaching time available for microeconomics as such alongside the greater demands placed upon what is taught and how (beyond the mainstream to include methodology, history of thought and heterodox alternatives).

Essentially, what follows represents a lecture course of 20 hours with an almost exclusive focus upon theory as opposed to applied microeconomics whether empirically or policy oriented. In the past, I have often been encouraged by students and colleagues to write up my lecture notes as an alternative, heterodox textbook and, eventually, I have succumbed to this suggestion, at least in part. It has not been easy and not always rewarding because the intellectual challenges are more ones of expressing what you know clearly and precisely (if at times in tedious detail) rather than discovering something new for yourself and sharing it with others.

In addition, I would not describe what follows as an alternative or heterodox microeconomics textbook. I am far from convinced that such a volume is possible or even desirable, as if an atheist is tasked with constructing an alternative god and corresponding religion. As, hopefully, will become apparent, mainstream economics is deeply flawed, in part because of its substantive content but also because of its very goal – of constructing an understanding of a holistic economic system on the basis of the aggregated behaviour of atomistic individuals. Rather than offering a textbook of microeconomics, what follows is a presentation of the mainstream from a critical, heterodox perspective with some presentation of alternatives on the issues covered. These alternatives inevitably proceed from the macro to the micro, rather than vice versa, with a much broader understanding of the macro itself, as the social and the non-economic, rather than the simple sum of economic magnitudes.

In short, to understand the micro there is surely a need to understand what capitalism and capital are at an abstract level prior to examining how it operates at lower levels of detail. Of course, it might be claimed that if you want to understand mainstream microeconomics, you ought to go to a mainstream economist or at least a standard text. I do not doubt that this is in part correct, and there are plenty of texts from which to choose, at various levels of depth, breadth and difficulty (and the reader is encouraged to find one that best suits, with the two texts of Hal Varian being a good starting point). I have gone out of my way to present the mainstream as faithfully as it presents itself, if not necessarily in the way that would be welcomed by its practitioners. For, just as a priest might be the best person to explain religious doctrine (although for many this might mean confinement to a male viewpoint), so the non-believer's account is also of merit, drawing on an outsider's perspective and highlighting what is not there as much as what is there.

This means that the elaboration of the mainstream here is heavily complemented by criticism, something that the reader may find irksome. But, as the narrator's father suggests at the beginning of the Great Gatsby:

Whenever you feel like criticizing anyone … just remember that all the people in this world haven't had the advantages that you've had.

Well, nothing could be truer in the case of mainstream economics relative to heterodoxy. It has the disadvantages of being ignorant and negligent of methodology, history of economic thought, realism, genuine interdisciplinarity and alternative approaches. But these disadvantages are both self-imposed and positively embraced, and complemented by the overwhelming advantage of what almost constitutes an institutionalised monopoly over the discipline of economics. As a result, the case for critical presentation of the mainstream could not be stronger.

I want to thank, if not in name, those who commented on the text at various stages in its preparation. Thanks too to the team at Pluto, and especially Dan Harding for his meticulous copy-editing. Most of all, though, thanks to the students who have borne the burden of teaching me what to teach them and how best to attempt to do so.

For an account of the 'superiority of economists', see Fourcade et al. (2015). See also Fine (2011a) for the prospects for alternatives given this 'superiority'.

Ben Fine is Professor of Economics at the School of Oriental and African Studies, University of London, and holds honorary positions at the Universities of Johannesburg (Senior Research Fellow attached to the South African Research Chair in Social Change), Rhodes University (Visiting Professor, Institute of Social and Economic Research), and Witswatersrand (Associate Researcher, Corporate Strategy and Industrial Development).

1

Locating Microeconomics

1.1 Overview

The purpose of this chapter is to provide a specification of the nature of mainstream microeconomics in a number of ways, not least by locating it within the history of economic thought (Section 1.2). In part, understanding the nature of microeconomics is aided by understanding its origins and history.

First, not necessarily following it in chronological order, is to trace how microeconomics got to be the way that it is, presenting its journey from the marginalist revolution of the 1870s to the formalist revolution of the 1950s (Sections 1.3 and 1.5).

Second is to describe each of these revolutions. The marginalist revolution brought into play many of the concepts that are now taken for granted within the mainstream. It also involved the break with classical political economy with which it is contrasted across a number of key elements (Section 1.3). The formalist revolution took off from the marginalist revolution, elevating the role of mathematics within economics (Section 1.6). Together these two revolutions underpinned the creation of what will be termed both a technical apparatus, of production and utility functions, and a technical architecture, of general equilibrium, both of which are more fully explained and explored in subsequent chapters.

Third is to pinpoint how, following the formalist revolution, the technical apparatus and architecture have been decisive in expanding the influence of microeconomics over both economics as a whole (even incorporating macroeconomics) and across other social sciences and topics in a process that is termed here the (historical logic of) economics imperialism (Section 1.7). In short, from very narrow foundations with limited scope of application – individual optimisation for given utility and production functions in order to specify market supply and demand – microeconomics has become almost unlimited in scope.

Fourth is to highlight in more detail the so-called reductionism characteristic of mainstream economics. This ranges from its narrow and flawed methodological content, which is increasingly unwitting and uncritically taken for granted, through its highly unrealistic conceptualisations and assumptions from the perspective of other social sciences, and even to the technical assumptions within its own framework that are essential for the technical apparatus and architecture to prevail, (Section 1.4).

Fifth, the result is that microeconomics today has a schizophrenic relationship to its origins in the marginalist revolution of the 1870s. On the one hand, it remains securely founded on the core principle of individual optimisation and the core concepts of utility and production functions, efficiency and equilibrium. It is equally centred on supply and demand and the determination of market prices and quantities. On the other hand, it has become prodigiously promiscuous and even incoherent in its incorporation of whatever other factors and subject matter take its fancy, especially where these are amenable to mathematical modelling and econometric investigation. This reveals the intellectual and analytical weaknesses of the mainstream – its inability to explain its primary subject matter, the economy, on the basis of its core principles and concepts so that it has to introduce extraneous material to rescue itself. On the other hand, this is also to reveal the disciplinary strength and stranglehold of the mainstream. So secure are its principles that it is able to project them wherever it pleases with whatever it pleases. In an Appendix to this chapter, some discussion is offered on how economists might defend what they do although, in practice, this is often arbitrary and far from deeply considered.

1.2 Microeconomics as History of Economic Thought

Textbooks in microeconomics generally begin with the optimising behaviour of individuals. Consumers, sometimes understood to represent households despite their composition of varieties of individuals and possibly conflicting interests, are presumed to maximise their utility, or preference level, subject to prevailing prices. This gives rise to demand for consumer goods and supply of labour (subject to any other assets that may be held). Firms maximise profits contingent on the technologies available to them and prices at which they can buy inputs and sell outputs.

Such consumer and producer behaviour is dealt with in Chapters 2 and 3, respectively. There, as will be seen in more detail, whilst economics and economists have become unquestioningly habituated to such framing of micro-economics, at least as a starting point, doing so involves a series of serious oversights that it is the purpose of this chapter to highlight.

First is to recognise that microeconomics as such is of a relatively recent vintage. Indeed, it is nominally less than a hundred years old, with the major division of the discipline of economics into the two fields of microeconomics and macroeconomics only explicitly emerging in the 1930s as macro, especially in the form of Keynesianism, sought to deal with the mass unemployment attached to the Great Depression. This is, of course, to enter the domain of the history of economic thought, something that modern microeconomics (and economics more generally) has studiously overlooked. Nor is delving into the history of our discipline simply to provide a narrative of what came before and when, possibly with the presumption that the theory just got better and better, building on what has gone before, especially with the increasing adoption of mathematical techniques. As will become apparent, the results of situating microeconomics historically are much more extensive, rewarding and challenging. We gain the prospect of learning why the theory emerges as it does, when it does, with what scope of application and with what content. And we can also draw lessons concerning the nature of microeconomics as it is today.

Such issues might be understood in terms of a sociology of knowledge; why does microeconomics emerge and evolve as it does? There are at least two broad approaches to such questions. The first or 'absolute' approach places emphasis on the internal development of the discipline itself as it raises and solves problems of its own making. The second or 'relative' approach suggests that external influences play a role in theory development, although these may be due to circumstances (was Keynesianism a response to mass unemployment?) or to vested interests, ideological or otherwise (was monetarism a response to, and/or support for, neoliberalism and/or financial interests?).

A choice does not need to be made between the absolute and relative approaches if accepting that external and internal influences mutually interact and condition one another. It is usually, however, much easier to trace the logical development of a discipline than to explain how external influences encouraged, or allowed, such development to be generated and accepted. This would require a detailed examination of what was going on in the economy, politics and ideology, as well as the institutions of higher learning.

1.3 From Marginalist Revolution ...

Such a task is beyond our account of microeconomics other than to emphasise that its history and content are not reducible to the strengthening of an irrefutable body of theory that was simply waiting to be discovered and refined for the modern textbook. Ways of seeing the microeconomy are as much open to dispute as they are to discovery – or amnesia! And, not only in name is microeconomics a new arrival on the scene, deriving from the 1930s. For the principles underpinning microeconomics were established only 50 years or so earlier during what is known as the marginalist revolution of the 1870s. The moniker 'marginalist' derives from the idea that optimisation (for example of consumer or producer decisions) will have been achieved when a small, or 'marginal', change in some decision (for example, how much to produce or consume), leaves the optimiser no better off, everything else remaining the same (or *ceteris paribus*). The margin as such is usually captured by differentiating giving rise in particular to marginal cost, product or utility.

It is also worth rehearsing what was involved in this marginalist 'revolution', partly because many students never even get to learn about it so neglected is the teaching of the history of their discipline, and partly because it did establish the broad principles that govern the economics of today as opposed to how economics was conceived previously. A revolution involves a before, an after and a transition between the two. Prior to the marginalist revolution, economics as we understand it now was dominated by what is termed classical political economy, around which figures such as Adam Smith, David Ricardo, John Stuart Mill and Karl Marx loom large (although there are many differences amongst even these few representatives). Following the revolution, there was established mainstream, orthodox, neoclassical economics (I will use the terms interchangeably although mainstream most of the time), very much as we know it today. The transition between the two did not take place in a day, a year or a decade, but was extended across different issues over a number of decades before and after the 1870s (and it might be argued that the revolution began in the early nineteenth century and was only complete in the 1950s, see below).

This leads some to argue that there is no such thing as the marginalist revolution as such. But a simple comparison of before and after suggests otherwise across a number of elements. First, whilst the basic unit of analysis of microeconomics is the optimising individual, classical political economy focuses upon class relations, especially across capital, labour and land.

Second, microeconomics has a preoccupation with equilibrium. This is so even when it is dealing with (what is termed steady-state balance) growth of the economic system as a whole. By contrast, classical political economy is concerned with the processes of growth *and* change (not least because it is seeking to come to terms with what is the relatively new era of industrialisation with major economic and social impacts). Whilst microeconomics is concerned with static considerations, or at most stability, classical political economy addresses the historical and dynamic properties of the economic system.

Third, microeconomics is concerned with issues around the efficient use of given resources in the context of given production conditions. In this respect, it is ahistorical, tending to overlook the different economic and social relations under which such efficiency may or may not be generated (although presuming that market-type behaviour is universal wherever it can flourish). Classical political economy, on the other hand, is sensitive to different historically organised economic systems – after all, efficiency under feudalism or slavery is different than under capitalism.

Fourth, as today's students know only too well, microeconomics is based upon a deductive method: one makes some assumptions (optimising individuals) and draws out conclusions on this basis. Classical political economy is more inductive, seeking to base its theory on close empirical observation of society (such as its class nature).

Fifth, microeconomics bases its understanding of value (and price) on a subjective theory of value. Ultimately, what things are worth is what individuals are willing to pay for them at the margin of consumption (although this is a subjectivity of the individual that is very different from postmodernism, in which subjectivity is invented, bound up with forging of identity, etc., as opposed to being given by a utility function). Classical political economy is more committed to an objective theory of value, one based on cost of production independent of demand, especially drawing upon the labour theory of value in which labour time to produce something underpins its value.

Last, microeconomics is intradisciplinary to the extreme, with its principles far removed from the concerns of other social science disciplines (with their preoccupation, for example, not only with class but also power, conflict and ideology). Classical political economy is very different, not least as signified by its name, embedding its understanding of the economy into broader economic and social factors beyond the market, and not confining itself to what has become the traditional subject matter of economics.

1.4 ... Through Methodology ...

As is at least implicit in what has gone before, microeconomics adopts a stance on certain methodological issues. It chooses methodological individualism (of a special type, utility maximisation as opposed to broader behavioural or motivational determinants – as in psychology for example) over methodological holism (the study of the system as a whole prior to the study of its individual components); deduction (and especially mathematical technique) over induction; an intradisciplinary over an interdisciplinary approach; and an ahistorical or universal methodology (applicable at all times, places and circumstances without regard to history and context) over theory attuned to the specific nature of the object under study (such as capitalism as opposed to slavery). In addition, previously explicitly if less so more recently, microeconomics presumes a separation between positive and normative theory, between what is and what ought to be, presuming that its principles are ethically neutral, or value-free, whether right or wrong.

This separation is acknowledged by some philosophers to be unobtainable, not least because how we express things inevitably incorporates some ethical content – compare the notion of production as a relationship between inputs and outputs with its being understood as a class relationship of exploitation. By the same token, the presumption that evidence can be given independently from theory as the basis on which to test theories is also false – we need at least a conceptual framework to determine how we construct evidence: what does or does not count as a component part of GDP or the unemployed for example.

Each of these issues around methodology is extremely controversial. Whilst it is possible to discuss each issue separately, it is not at all clear that they can be settled in isolation from one another, nor that everyone will agree on the nature of the methodology. Any methodology is almost certainly liable to incorporate a complex mix across these separate elements but not necessarily be defined by that mix, even with added ingredients. But what stands out about microeconomics is the extent to which it adopts an extreme position on each and every element. The point here is not so much to demonstrate that this is unacceptable (both in principle and in practice) from the perspectives of the study of methodology and of other social sciences (and, indeed, of the physical sciences with which economics often seeks to compare itself) – the market system cannot come from individuals, and nor can the language with which we engage in it, let alone discuss it; the market system cannot be isolated from society; it cannot be discussed with value-free concepts; it cannot be based on deductive principles alone (where do concepts such as the optimising individual come from in the first place?); and it cannot be assessed on the basis of externally given data. Rather, to reiterate, the point is to observe the extremes to which microeconomics has been driven methodologically and, subsequently, to reveal how this relates to the substantive content of the theory involved.

For, with the marginalist revolution based on the optimising individual (with utility or production function as consumer or producer, respectively), two important goals were established for what was to become designated as micro-economics. The first was to focus upon the economy as market relations, with the otherwise corresponding neglect of the social, the historical and the insti-tutional. Thus, microeconomics became concentrated on supply and demand. This involved one sort of 'reductionism', a narrowing of the understanding of what is the economic and what factors comprise and determine it. The second goal involved a second type of reductionism, not only to the individual, as already indicated, but also to that individual as 'rational' in the sense of being committed – pure and simple – to the pursuit of self-interest. Homo economicus, or economic rationality, became identified even more narrowly with utility maximisation as the sole factor in individual motivation and behaviour.

To some extent, at least in principle, the focus upon such rationality can be seen as a reasonable response to the emergence of the market itself as the major form taken by economic relations. Surely, this does itself inspire a particular form of motivation and behaviour across individuals even if in other areas of our lives we might be more rounded, irrational even, as human beings in going about our daily business as citizens and family members. Nonetheless, rightly or wrongly, microeconomics became concerned with the notion of (economic) rationality in the sense discussed, with a presumption that other forms of behaviour, especially in market relations, should be lumped together as 'irrational'. Such a pejorative term suggested by implication that such behaviour should be left to other disciplines, and is liable to be unsystematic, not of great significance, and subject to erosion by competitive processes (if more so in the arena of production than consumption).

1.5 ... To Implosion onto TA²

Such predispositions towards focusing upon economic rationality in this form in the context of market relations almost inevitably gave rise to the posing of a particular problem for microeconomics. Given economic rationality, what are the implications for (individual) supply and demand? Does supply inevitably increase with price, and demand decrease? And, even more formally, what are the mathematical implications for supply and demand curves given that they are derived from the optimising behaviour of individuals?

The solution to these problems is discussed in some detail in Chapters 2 and 3, on consumer and producer theory, respectively. For the moment, though, the first point to emphasise is that this is the problem microeconomics sets itself. The second point is that microeconomics is single-mindedly prepared to make any sacrifices – or, on its own terms if rarely put this way, to make whatever assumptions are necessary – to generate a solution.

These sacrifices are, indeed, prodigious. For example, as already indicated for the consumer, this is an individual with fixed preferences over fixed goods, with a single motivation and behaviour. As a result, goods carry no meaning other than their physical properties, and individuals have no subjectivity other than a given utility function, and so are stripped of the possibility of making their own identity (free to choose as consumers but predetermined through their utility functions in what they will choose and what utility is given by those choices). Differences between individuals, let alone their individuality or its making, are obliterated. There are no differences, by nation, region, gender, race, ethnicity and so on, nor by motives – all are simply driven by given utility. Of course, other (non-individualistic) approaches also obliterate some or all of these differences at the outset – those addressing class or gender, for example, especially where these are analytically or causally privileged as opposed to the individual. But, what is peculiar about this abstraction or assumption in mainstream economics is that it is the individual that is being addressed as the privileged concept, but without any individuality.

Further, even within this framework, as students at all levels soon recognise and to which they become habituated, certain technical assumptions are necessary for the problems of determining supply and demand to be resolved. In elementary terms, quite apart from effectively eliminating time and space from the analysis, these simplifying assumptions include diminishing marginal utility, for example, in order that orderly mathematical solutions can be derived for the utility-maximising consumer. Such assumptions are not and cannot be motivated by any reference to empirical evidence, but are the consequence of what is necessary for the theory. As it were, as so often within economics, the world must fit the theory and, if it does not do so, so much the worse for the world. And, having sinned once or thrice in making its assumptions, the mainstream simply carries on without a second thought other than convenience to the theoretical (or possibly other purposes, such as to ease the undertaking of empirical work or to be able to come to and/or support particular policy conclusions).

Of course, in this and other contexts, this very appropriately raises the issue of the 'realism' of microeconomics (and economics more generally). Now realism is itself a very tricky notion and is highly controversial (as much so as methodology), and is open to many different positions with different elements and possible combinations. It involves both *ontology* (what is the nature of reality – is it like a set of equations or a mathematical model, is it the same for the physical as for the social world, and what room is there for uncertainty as opposed to regularity in outcomes, even beyond probabilistic understandings?), and *epistemology* (what is the nature of our knowledge of the world; moreover, do we get that knowledge through observation or reasoning, and how do we know whether we are right or wrong?).

As with methodology, it is beyond this text to cover debates on ontology and epistemology. Rather, once again, the purpose is more to highlight how extreme is the position to which microeconomics is pushed. As it were, it is the needs of the theory that are in command at the expense of everything else, including realism however this is understood. It has become extremely rare for micro-economists especially (but economists more generally) even to decipher and recognise, let alone justify, their positions in these respects and how they differ from, and even are thought to be invalid from, the perspectives of other social sciences and those who specialise in methodology.

To some extent, these and other issues may have been acknowledged, if set aside, as microeconomics was being established and strengthened. But today, with microeconomic theory as part of the conventional wisdom of the discipline, the presumption is that there is some underlying methodology and notion of realism that can support it. What is informally involved is some combination of deductive reasoning from axioms which is taken to be indisputable (maths done properly cannot be wrong) together with some form of falsifiability (well, if our axioms are wrong, this will show up in our conclusions and will be invalidated by empirical testing).

Both in principle and in practice, these positions are known to be wrong. As already mentioned, it is impossible to construct evidence, for example, without preconceptions; and it is almost impossible to refute a theory through evidence (and it rarely happens in economics) because it can generally be modified to take account of apparent empirical anomalies. For example, if estimates of demand do not fit we can always claim the theory is still correct but the underlying utility functions may have shifted.

Otherwise, critics of (micro)economics often point to its undue reliance upon mathematics. To some degree, this is misplaced. There is nothing wrong with mathematical reasoning. It can both clarify our arguments and it can even be used as a tool to discover and present results that are not otherwise apparent. But there are limitations on the form and content that can be taken by mathematical reasoning. It has difficulty dealing with aggregates such as power, class and conflict, or even the state and concepts such as liquidity that involve beliefs and ideology. As emphasised, though, mathematical reasoning fits extremely comfortably with the directions taken by microeconomics, but that is the fault of the theory not of mathematics as such.

By the same token, it is worth observing that, despite its claims for rigour because of its use of mathematics in theory and evidence in testing, and a corresponding claim of being parallel with the methods of the (natural) sciences, this is not true (and nor is it appropriate, since economics concerns the social not the physical world so that their methods are justifiably and necessarily different from one another). The physical sciences do use mathematical reasoning and modelling and they do test theories against the evidence. And yet, those who study the methodology of science would be appalled at the naïve and extreme postures of microeconomics. In any case, the theories and hypotheses that are used in the natural sciences are heavily influenced by close empirical observation as opposed to the more or less arbitrary assumptions attached to microeconomics (especially concerning the individual which we know are not and cannot be true) that are driven by its own inner goals as opposed to correspondence with its object of study.

In addition, as mentioned, microeconomics has heavily involved a reductionism towards a particular type of individual behaviour in the context of market supply and demand. In many respects, in what will be termed an 'implosion' upon its core methods and assumptions, this resulted in the throwing away of those considerations that got in the way of deriving the desired results. It became a matter of teasing out as full a set of implications as possible from individual optimising behaviour, irrespective of the assumptions necessary to do so. A further consequence has been to consolidate the division between (micro)economics and other disciplines to which, from its own perspective, were allocated issues related to non-economic or irrational behaviour and social factors whether related to the non-market or to the non-individual (institutions, politics, ideology, the law and so on, even though these are recognisably prerequisites for the market and affect its functioning). And, especially in the interwar period, whilst the core results of microeconomics were being established, there was a strong separation between it and economics more generally. It was as if the discipline indulged the exercise in implosion on its own narrow terrain whilst continuing to go about its own, more important business of studying how the economy as a whole functioned.

At the time, institutional economics and applied economics of various types and economic history were particularly strong, with a heavy reliance upon inductive methods – analysing the rise of monopolies and trade unions, the patterns and causes of business cycles, the changing distribution of income and wealth, etc. Significantly, by the time of the Great Depression nobody looked to microeconomics to explain massive unemployment. As a result, (Keynesian) macroeconomics emerged alongside microeconomics although, unsurprisingly, there were those who argued that too high real wages were the cause of unemployment on grounds that would be instantly recognisable to standard microeconomics. Whilst, in the early 1930s and in the context of massive unemployment, Lionel Robbins sought to define economics as the allocation of scarce resources between competing ends, this had to wait a couple of decades before it was more readily accepted.

By the 1950s, the goals that microeconomics had eventually set itself had been accomplished. The first (already discussed), of drawing out the implications of individual optimisation, gives rise to the Slutsky–Hicks–Samuelson conditions (see Chapter 2). These provide the necessary and sufficient conditions for (individual) supply and demand curves to have been derived from optimisation. But there was a second goal that came to prominence later, in contrast to the partial equilibrium analysis of the marginalist revolution that had been inspired by Alfred Marshall who laid out much of the conceptual and technical apparatus that is familiar to all students of economics (marginal cost, utility, externalities, monopoly pricing, consumer surplus, and so on). This is how to put such individual supply and demand curves together across the whole economy and find, in general equilibrium, what price vector would equate supply and demand for all markets simultaneously.

Kenneth Arrow and Gerard Debreu proved the existence of general equilibrium in the early 1950s. In effect, this is the ultimate achievement of microeconomics since it both rests upon individual optimisation and the aggregation over all individuals to form the economy as a whole. However, once again, the desire to forge a theory of general equilibrium involved an implosion of its own, albeit overlapping with that of individual optimisation. Apart from so-called perfectly competitive markets (in which all firms are taken to be price-takers, on which see Chapter 4), to guarantee the unique existence of a stable Pareto efficient general equilibrium required no increasing returns to scale, no externalities, and that all goods be more or less gross substitutes for each other (see Chapter 2) – as well as the standard methods and assumptions around individual optimisation.

By the 1950s, the microeconomic implosion was complete and gave rise to what has already been dubbed the technical apparatus and the technical architecture, or TA². The technical apparatus involves the optimising behaviour of individuals around utility functions, u, and productions functions, f. The technical architecture concerns the preoccupation with efficiency and equilibrium for the economy as a whole (or some part of it) on the basis of the technical apparatus. As emphasised, in the process of developing TA², an implosion was involved in reducing the analysis to one particular type of behaviour in the context of both special assumptions and methods and with a focus on market supply and demand alone.

1.6 From Implosion onto TA² to Explosion into Economics Imperialism

Such are the *historical* circumstances and conditions which allowed micro-economics to emerge and flourish, recognisably confined in scope to what was analytically incorporated, how it was incorporated and in corresponding range of application. But, somewhat perversely, the technical apparatus itself, whilst developed for and applied to market relations (in the form of supply and demand in response to prices), contained no such boundaries in principle. Precisely because they had been stripped of social and historical content, utility and production functions had become universal in application. They express what individuals want and how they produce it (possibly for others via the market) irrespective of circumstance, as if blaringly apparent in light of their formal expression in formal mathematical terms – the ubiquitous utility and production functions. Consequently, the *logic* of the technical apparatus is that it should be of universal applicability, even if the *historical* circumstances that inspired and allowed for its birth confined it to supply and demand upon the market alone.

As a result, there is a tension between the historically derived scope of application of microeconomics and its logical potential (at least on its own terms), something that can be dubbed its historical logic. The history points to an implosion but the logic goes in the opposite, explosive direction with no presumption of confinement of microeconomics to the market alone, nor even to the economy alone, equally giving rise to what is termed economics imperialism by its proponents as well as its critics.

For, having insulated itself within economics and from other social sciences, microeconomics finds itself with the potential to expand its scope of application across both its host discipline and other disciplines and topics other than market supply and demand (and, as will be seen, beyond optimising individuals, aggregated or otherwise). To what extent it does so, by way of parody, depends upon what might be thought of as intellectual supply and demand. But, having been reduced to TA², with general equilibrium as its pinnacle, how far the historical logic moves in favour of the logic and against the initial history of its foundation depends upon the efforts of microeconomists, on the one hand (the supply), and how these efforts are received by fellow economists and other social scientists, on the other (the demand).

In short, the historical logic of microeconomics dictates that at first it should implode upon TA^2 before reversing direction and exploding across both economics and the social sciences more generally. In part, this involved consolidating TA^2 as a core element within economics as a discipline (as the science of supply and demand upon the market), something that rapidly occurred in the post-war period with the standardised division between macroeconomics and microeconomics, complemented by a whole range of other, mainly applied fields and specialisations for which, like macroeconomics, the core TA^2 was perceived to be inappropriate. In addition, in the post-war period, in what has been termed a formalist revolution – one shared by both microeconomics and macroeconomics – the mathematical representation of economic principles evolved from being uncommon to standard and, ultimately, more or less required (with econometrics as the way to deploy evidence following on not far behind).

As a result, at least initially, the expansion in the application of microeconomic principles was limited rather than slow. Its main successes were with: economic history (or cliometrics as it came to be known, with the abolition of slavery for example treated as if it were the consequence of individual profit maximisation); with human capital theory (that different skills should be treated as inputs and outputs more or less like any others, see Chapter 6); and with public choice theory (the treatment of politics as if underpinned by utility maximisation and, most infamously, the idea that choosing between war and peace is comparable to choosing between apples and pears).

Such economics imperialism was, though, limited in terms of scope and acceptability by a number of factors. First, microeconomics remained subordinate to macroeconomics in the hierarchy of the two fields, and macroeconomics remained aloof within Keynesian analysis from reliance upon TA^2, despite being formalised within the standard textbook IS/LM framework that dominated macroeconomics during the post-war boom (see counterpart volume, *Macroeconomics: A Critical Companion*). Second, by the same token, economists were conscious by virtue of training and disposition, in part from applied economics, not to reduce broader issues to the same principles as those determining supply and demand within or across individuals and individual markets. Nonetheless, macroeconomics did on occasion, very fully and early on, succumb in piecemeal fashion to the far from subtle charms of microeconomics, especially with the use of production functions to represent supply for the economy as a whole, most notably in growth theory from the mid-1950s (which explains why consideration of the aggregate production function, a macro topic, appears in this micro text, see Chapter 5). Third, in particular, it seemed entirely appropriate to reject the notion that non-market issues should be determined by an analysis that presumed an as-if market theory and, in general, one in which such markets worked more or less perfectly. In addition, the post-war boom, underpinned by extensive and growing state intervention (perceived as Keynesian/welfarism/modernisation) was hardly conducive to individualistic analysis within economics let alone across the other social sciences.

Nonetheless, economics imperialism did make some progress, and established a significant foothold within the discipline (all three leading applications mentioned were eventually acknowledged by a number of Nobel Prizes for the leading economists responsible for them). Essentially, something perverse, even incoherent, was occurring. TA^2 could only be established by taking out a whole range of considerations: from the social to the historical, from the nature of individuals to the nature of goods, and even from externalities and the like to narrow technical assumptions concerning diminishing returns. As a result, TA^2 was necessarily extremely vulnerable to criticism of omission of serious considerations in establishing itself. It can only have limited applicability according to the conditions (possibly empty) in which its assumptions hold or, at least, in which they are perceived to be sufficiently weighty to justify overlooking other considerations.

Yet, having omitted these factors to be able to establish itself, in shifting from implosion to explosion, economics imperialism began to use TA^2 to analyse the very factors that it had been necessary to exclude to establish itself. As it were, we exclude politics to create TA^2, then we use TA^2 to analyse politics. This process is one of bringing back in (BBI) – a key component of economics imperialism – and it is worth taking a closer look at its elementary and initial stages. Precisely because of BBI, it has been argued that microeconomics in particular, and economics in general, is now immune from criticisms that it excludes the political, the institutional, the social and the historical because they are now part and parcel of its analysis.

Although this was not acknowledged as such initially – it was less a matter of BBI than of simple extension of TA^2 to new pastures – there is necessarily a grain of truth in this claim. BBI is highly characteristic of economics today on an extensive scale, for reasons which will emerge. Almost any topic and factor can be found addressed within economics, as is evident from the appearance, and popularity, of books with titles like the economic theory of everything and most notably with *Freakonomics*. Significantly, look for a definition of institutions within economics, and the new institutional economics, and you will find it is defined more or less as everything else that is not already incorporated into TA^2 (much the same is true of social capital that has become a hit within economics as well as other disciplines as an umbrella term for everything that might otherwise have been excluded). However, this all-inclusiveness does not negate the dependence of such BBI upon TA^2 that was itself dependent on the original taking out. As a result, BBI by economics is marked by two important characteristics. One is conceptual inconsistency – examine an individual's changing preferences, for example, on the basis of a TA² in which preferences are taken as fixed.

This is not the same, as might be argued, as the assumption in mechanics of frictionless motion, or within a vacuum, from which we might proceed to address the effect of friction. After all, we always need simplifying assumptions as a theoretical starting point, although what these are and how they are made should be justified. For example, we do not attempt to understand friction on the basis of its non-existence, even if we try to understand other things on this basis. So we might understand the impact of politics as a friction on supply and demand, but we cannot use supply and demand constructed in the absence of politics to tell us what politics is and what it does. That is unless, as a second characteristic, we privilege TA² as prime causal determinant of everything, a position to which economics imperialism is inevitably drawn. This is, however, arbitrary, extreme and wrong for reasons already argued around methodology, and, in any case, it ultimately offers little or no explanation at all. It is simply a tautology to interpret the world as being the result of individuals optimising given utility functions, which they themselves can change if optimal to do so, and subject to whatever preferences they might have had in the first place.

This discussion is becoming somewhat tangential to the task of charting the evolution of microeconomics. It is possibly justified on the grounds that when push comes to shove, mainstream economists do tend to defend themselves on the grounds that this is simply what they do as economists as opposed to other disciplines and/or that individual preferences and their satisfaction are the fundamentals in understanding the economy as a whole if not the broader world. That economists have come to believe this is so is relatively new, even within the brief historical span of microeconomics.

1.7 From Old to New Economics Imperialism

And the belief has become stronger, even predominant over much else within the discipline. In this respect, the collapse of the post-war boom, and of Keynesianism in the 1970s and its displacement by monetarism, are extremely important in three ways. First, although not of immediate concern to our account of microeconomics as such, the rise of monetarism and, ultimately, its passage to the new classical economics, heavily consolidated the presence of microeconomics within the discipline, as macroeconomics became based upon the optimising behaviour of individuals (including their – rational – expectation formation). The so-called microfoundations of macroeconomics clearly signalled the success of economics imperialism within its home discipline, switching microeconomic theory to a position of precedence over macroeconomics. Second, the rise of neoliberalism encouraged a correspond-ing extension of microeconomic principles to what had previously been the insulated and more inductive applied and policy branches of the discipline, from industrial through to development economics.

Third, and most important of all, was less the galloping success of economics imperialism on the grounds of extending microeconomic principles on the basis of as if perfectly working markets but in the partial reaction against this in its most extreme form. This original, old-style phase of economics imperialism was supplemented, or even displaced, by a new phase in which emphasis was placed not on treating non-market factors as if they could be analysis as if equivalent to a perfectly working market, but on the non-market understood as the consequence of, or response to, imperfectly working markets. Most significant in this shift, then, has been the appeal to market imperfections, especially asymmetric information.

Precisely because it is built upon the notion that markets work imperfectly, this new development within microeconomics represents a critical departure from neoliberal ideology in the sense of pure support for laissez-faire. But it is equally important to emphasise how it totally accepts TA^2 as its analytical foundations (and within macroeconomics it also tends to accept rational expectations). Despite this, and its corresponding commitment to methodological individualism, it is able to produce some remarkable results on the simple premise that some individuals come to market with different information than others.

First, as mentioned, is that markets do not work perfectly. Second, for details of which see Chapter 6, these imperfections can take one of three forms – markets may clear (i.e. supply equal demand) but be (Pareto) inefficient (someone could ideally be made better off without anyone else being made worse off); markets may not clear (supply and demand do not equal but prices do not move, so there are trades that could be made that would be mutually beneficial); and markets might not be formed at all (ditto). Third, especially in light of the latter two possible outcomes, even though the economics is based upon the optimising behaviour of *individuals*, it is able to explain the presence of *structures* rather than, as in other economic approaches and social sciences, structures are taken as given as the basis to explain what individuals can or cannot do. This is because, for example, if the labour market does not clear (wages do not fall even though there is unemployment, essentially because employers want more loyal, productive, conscientious employees and can only guarantee this through a higher wage than they need to pay, with the extra wage costs more than worth it in terms of profitability), there is generated (and not assumed), a structural division between the employed and the unemployed, with no reason for the wage to fall.

Such reasoning does not apply exclusively to the labour markets – it is of general applicability. With these three possible outcomes (and perfectly working, efficient markets as a special case), asymmetric information economics is able to offer an explanation for, possibly inefficient, market structures throughout

the economy (and at the macroeconomic level too, restoring Keynesian macroeconomics on microfoundations in its own image). But nor is it simply economic
structures and their corresponding inefficiencies that are addressed. These do
themselves form the basis for explaining non-market factors, for they can be
seen as providing the rationale for non-market, possibly collective, behaviour
to correct market imperfections. The classic example of this is Akerlof's market
for 'lemons' (the secondhand car market). Asymmetric information means that
better cars cannot trade at a premium and poorer cars at a discount so that
the market works imperfectly (because buyers cannot distinguish them). It
makes sense for legitimate dealers to set up a warranty, i.e. non-market, system.
Such a parable is an indicative proxy for all non-market outcomes and, most
dramatically, to explain the existence of the state as the biggest corrector of
market failures of them all.

However, the extent of interventionism associated with this new microeconomics should not be exaggerated. It is piecemeal and contingent upon
the extent to which there are market imperfections and whether intervention
(still motivated by individual gain by those forming and acting through such
intervention) leads to better outcomes than without them. This is of lesser
concern here than in observing the extent to which the new asymmetric
information microeconomics (again, attracting a flush of Nobel Prizes for
Economics) heavily advanced the cause of economics imperialism. It did so on
the sides of both supply and demand. On the supply side, the notion of market
imperfections as an explanation for both economic and social structures opened
up an almost unlimited terrain of applications for economic principles. As far as
other social sciences are concerned, on the demand side the departure from as-if
perfectly working markets, and the sudden dramatic discovery by economists
that institutions, and structures more generally, matter considerably, added to
the appeal of economics imperialism.

This new phase of economics imperialism, taking its cue from the old as a
critical point of departure through the introduction of market imperfections,
had the effect of rejuvenating the old applications as well as introducing a
whole range of new fields, often with the moniker 'new' attached – the new
development economics, the new economic sociology, the new institutional
economics, the new welfare economics, the new economic history, the new
financial economics, and so on. It is worth reiterating that the corresponding
widening scope of application both within economics itself and in colonising
the subject matter of other social science, continued to rely upon TA^2 despite the
processes of BBI what had been left out to establish it in the first place.

To some extent, this signified an extraordinary, if implicit, confession of
weakness on the part of microeconomics over and above the conceptual inconsistencies involved. For it was to accept that microeconomic principles in and of
themselves are insufficient to explain the economy, and that other factors have

to be incorporated to do this (even if appropriating the subject matter involved on the basis of TA^2). As mentioned above, 'institutions', for example, become a proxy for explaining everything that was not previously explained. And the more mainstream economics addresses the subject matter of other disciplines, the more it exposes itself to criticism for the narrow reductionism of its methods, theories and concepts from the perspectives of those other disciplines.

However, the mirror image of such weakness has been the consolidation of the status of TA^2 itself. Whatever the problem, our starting point can always be utility and production functions, and preoccupation with individual optimisation, efficiency and equilibrium. In addition, increasing reliance upon mathematical modelling has been at the expense of conceptual considerations, the meaning of categories of analysis both to modellers themselves as well as to the economic agents whom they model. Such concerns have been notable as no-go areas in the general trend towards BBI, as they cannot be accommodated within TA^2. And much the same is true of concepts such as power and conflict although these too can, if uncomfortably, be reduced to fit into models based on TA^2.

Paradoxically, though, this double weakness of microeconomics – its need both to rely upon factors outside of its immediate compass and its introduction of these factors inconsistently or incoherently with TA^2 – also endows it with considerable strength in scope of application. For, as these weaknesses become habituated, they go unnoticed and unremarked, and it becomes commonplace simply to presume that TA^2 is of universal application with or without the addition of other approaches or factors with which it is mutually compatible or not. It is as if TA^2 can be suspended to suit the incorporation of whatever explanatory element is more or less arbitrarily chosen. This was not always the case, especially during the first phase of economics imperialism where there was at least some consistent insistence upon reducing everything to TA^2. Subsequently, other than in its disciplinary prestige, TA^2 itself is arbitrary as a privileged starting point for allowing for other factors, but nonetheless it remains privileged within the discipline (although some would argue that its predominance is being eroded).

As a result, the ideas of satisficing behaviour or bounded rationality were rejected as microeconomics was attaining its status within the discipline – if they had been accepted before TA^2 was sufficiently secure, this would have questioned its acceptability. Similarly, techniques such as game theory were not initially adopted by microeconomics since it involves strategising and taking a view on what other people's preferences (and views) might be, and so preferences would be contingent on those of others rather than exogenously given. Today, especially in the wake of the 2008 financial crisis which seemed to put TA^2 into question, microeconomics is much more open to incorporating other explanatory factors, especially those associated with behavioural economics of one sort or another, even though these were previously subject to more or less total neglect, if not hostility, by microeconomics.

In short, microeconomics and economics imperialism have entered a third phase, following or, more exactly, supplementing one based on as-if perfectly working markets and one based on as-if imperfectly working markets, with both of these relying exclusively on TA^2. Currently, the scope of explanatory ingredients and of their application has been extended even further by allowing both for TA^2 and for other factors to be incorporated in what is more or less a theoretical mish-mash but in which TA^2 still retains a privileged position.

1.8 Further Thoughts and Readings

This chapter draws very heavily upon Fine and Milonakis (2009) and Milonakis and Fine (2009), where a broad account is offered of the avenues discarded by mainstream economics in its development and elevation of microeconomics. See also the classic Heilbroner (2000). A wide-ranging account of the putative microfoundations of macroeconomics is to be found in King (2012). I have sought to locate the ethical content of mainstream economics in Fine (2013a), bearing in mind that it construes the economy and society in terms of the optimising behaviour of individuals more or less harmoniously coordinated through the market. The shifting nature of economics imperialism, in Kuhnian scientific revolution terms, is assessed in Fine (2004). For the role of mathematics in economics, see Fine (2011b) in the context of methodological individualism and Bigo and Negru (2014) in the wake of the global crisis. See also Chick and Dow (2001) and Dow (1998). For economics' 'physics envy', see Mirowski (1989). Lawson (2003) criticises the mainstream for its ontology from the perspective of critical realism. Lee (2009) offers an account of heterodox alternatives to the mainstream, as does Lee (2013) with a contribution on how it should relate to the mainstream and whether this should be seen as disintegrating in light of what has been described here as the latest phase of economics imperialism. For a popular exposition of the deficiencies of mainstream economics, and some alternatives, see Chang (2014). For alternative texts, see Keen (2011) and van Staveren (2014), and also Birks (2015) for some methodological issues.

1.9 Appendix: Can the Mainstream Be Defended?

There are at least three common defences for the deployment of TA^2 in microeconomics. One is to accept much of the criticism but to insist that the theory offers a first approximation or, to some degree, a core element of individual behaviour. In other words, the approach offers some level of realism. Another is to see all or parts of TA^2 as a standard against which to judge the real world by reference to that real world's divergences from that standard (maybe a bit like frictionless motion in the study of movement). Thus, behaviour can be accepted in reality as combining both rational and irrational elements, but TA^2 is concerned with the rational alone (as well as depending upon other assumptions that reflect lack of realism in order to create the standard, such as perfect competition and general equilibrium). A third defence, heavily promoted by Milton Friedman, is that the realism of assumptions is of no significance relative to whether a theory's empirical predictions prove valid or not.

These three rationalisations for TA^2 are not entirely consistent with one another. The first, for example, appeals to realism in some sense whereas the third totally rejects it. What they all share in common is that they have been mounted *ex post*, only once TA^2 was already in place. As suggested in this chapter, TA^2 derived from the implosion associated with solving particular problems posed by marginalism: what are the implications of individual optimisation and what are the consequences of aggregating such optimisation across individuals and markets? These goals prompted the emergence of TA^2, but not the wish to be realistic, to set a standard for all but irrational behaviour or to make correct empirical predictions. These latter motives may not have been entirely absent but they did not drive the theory. Rather, on the rare occasions when the standard assumptions and methods are questioned, usually by someone else and not self-criticism, there is a psychologically motivated knee-jerk reaction to defend them as opposed to placing them under genuine scrutiny. This is why much of what economists do is seen as bizarre from the perspective of other social sciences.

Interestingly, though, Alfred Marshall did wish to create a standard set of microeconomic principles that would capture the essence of the pursuit of self-interest through the market, but he saw such an 'organon', as he called it, as only a small part of individual behaviour and one less important than a richer set of motives and activities governing the economy and its prospects. But he also failed to translate such an organon into a theory of the working of the economy as a whole, relying upon partial as opposed to general equilibrium. Whilst the latter does fit the partial equilibrium parts together, for Marshall at least, it hardly began to capture the workings of the economy as a whole because of what is excluded.

More specifically, the first approach falters because the derivation of TA^2 inevitably departed realism in the assumptions made; it was not extracting core aspects of reality but deliberately, even arbitrarily, setting them aside in pursuit of its goals. Indeed, by way of analogy, examining climate change on the grounds that it is totally independent of human activity might be thought to be a good approximation as a starting point, but would tend to prove both wrong and an inappropriate starting point for dealing with the problems at hand. Much the same is surely true of given individual preferences, for example. The second approach cannot be justified as such without consideration of the content of its standard; why should TA^2 be privileged as standard, as opposed to the idea that God dictates the economy and reality is some divergence from this (see also Chapter 3, and the parallel between general equilibrium and the economy as understanding the horse by reference to the unicorn). A major problem with adopting deliberately unrealistic assumptions and testing them on the basis of empirical evidence is that the assumptions themselves would be rejected as the most immediate empirical consequence of the theory. Individual preferences are fixed – no they are not.

Of course, just because these rationalisations have primarily been launched *ex post* and are mutually inconsistent, this does not make them individually wrong (although we might look upon them with suspicion and beware defences that shift from one to the other for convenience). It should also be observed that these methodological defences tend to be casual, naïve and somewhat negligent of the literature on methodology and the much wider set of considerations it brings to bear (see Section 1.4 for some starters).

2
Elusive Consumers and the Theory of Demand

2.1 Overview

The theory of the consumer, and of demand, lies at the heart of mainstream economics, both because of its importance as a topic and because it is indicative of the broader nature of the mainstream. Yet, as shown in Section 2.2, its substantive content is extraordinarily limited in and of itself and in relation to the demands of the subject matter that it putatively addresses, and it has been like this for a very long time. Section 2.3, drawing on Chapter 1, seeks to explain why consumer theory got to be the way it is in terms of the problems that it set itself and how it went about solving them, laying out the basic content of the theory, not least in terms of the construction of the technical apparatus around the consumer. This leads, in Section 2.4, to a short discussion of the limitations of the theory on its own terms – how can such a reduced theory for the consumer and the consumed be projected into an understanding of aggregate consumption across the whole economy and across all goods? It cannot, except under very special assumptions. This is followed in Section 2.5 by an account of how and why consumer theory, despite its narrowness and deficiencies even on its own terms, has prodigiously expanded its scope of application both within economics and across other social sciences. Section 2.6 offers a broad sketch of an alternative approach to consumer theory – one that draws upon a political economy that, by contrast to the mainstream, is also necessarily and justifiably interdisciplinary. The final section discusses some of the wider implications of developments in and around consumer theory for the nature and prospects of economics as a discipline.

2.2 The Reduced Consumer

Putting aside a few technical developments, the consumer theory of orthodox, mainstream neoclassical economics today would be readily recognised and understood by the marginalist economists of the 1870s. Indeed, many of the concepts now used were first put forward and popularised by Alfred Marshall in his *Principles of Economics*. Published in 1891, it remained the main economics textbook for the next 50 years and ran to eight editions. When students in the twenty-first century learn of marginal utility and how relative marginal utilities should and would be equated to relative prices, they have a long tradition to support them. More advanced treatments at the highest levels of the discipline tend to be just that and not too much more. To go from school student to Nobel Prize winner in consumer theory, you would need to be a little more sophisticated technically but you would not need to be a lot more conceptually advanced. In this light, it is hardly surprising that there have been no Nobel Prize winners in Economics for consumer theory as such, for major advances in this field have been notable for their absence. Significantly, those Nobel Prizes that have been awarded with relevance for consumer behaviour have tended to question the legitimacy of the orthodoxy, usually nibbling at its margins rather than seeking major reconstruction, as with behavioural economics. This seems to be the only way to say something new, or at least different.

The unshifting and pervasive presence of neoclassical consumer theory is taken by its proponents to be indicative of its strength and veracity. It has become unquestioned analytical common sense and common wisdom within the discipline. How is the consumer to be treated? The answer is as an individual with a utility function (or, more generally, a set of preferences) that is to be maximised subject to constraints (prevailing prices and correspondingly available income). Yet, as will be shown below, the model of the consumer and of consumer behaviour is extraordinarily weak by reference to its lack of realism and its narrowness of scope in conceptualising the consumer, the consumed and consumption.

These bold critical assertions follow from the way in which the model (of the) consumer is constructed, being derived purely and simply from the utility function $u^i(x_1, x_2, x_3, ..., x_n)$ for the ith consumer and for the goods, $x_1, x_2, x_3, ..., x_n$. A number of points are immediately striking, not least that u^i is taken as exogenous, as given. How did individuals come to get the preferences that they have? For how long do they remain fixed? What would make them change? In the first, very long, instance at least, these issues are simply set aside. This gives rise to a paradox in how the individual (consumer) is constructed. For the consumer's actions are purely subjective, entirely personal and idiosyncratic, and given and fixed without reference to external (or internal, self-reflecting) influences. But, despite then relying exclusively upon the consumer's subjectivity (so much so that marginalism is denoted as a subjective theory of value), that subjectivity is reduced to almost nothing in its substantive content. The only thing that the subjective individual is permitted to do is to maximise a given utility function like an automaton. In short, the emphasis is upon individual subjectivity, but it is a predetermined and heavily reduced, if not non-existent, subjectivity. Individuals are positively encouraged to maximise their utility without any influence over what that utility is or could be made to be.

This lack of genuine subjectivity is reflected in four aspects. The first, as is already apparent, is in the narrowness of motivation and capabilities underpinning the consumer – utility maximisation takes precedence over everything else to the extent of their total exclusion. But, as is well known from other disciplines (from psychology, through marketing, to neuroscience) consumer behaviour is motivated and prompted by many different factors, whether conscious or not, and cannot be reduced to the single-minded hedonistic pursuit of given pleasures.

Second, more rounded individuals than the putative utility maximiser have the capacity to be *inventive* around their consumption. It is not purely a matter of receiving given goods but of creating pleasure and enjoyment out of them. Of course, advertisements are deployed to this end – not simply nor primarily to inform consumers of what goods are but what they might be with a little use of the consumer's (or advertiser's) imagination. This is so much so that advertisements appealing to lack of imagination ('it does what it says on the tin', for example, or 'this is the cheapest') stand out not only as exceptional but as ironic. This all positively points to the capacity of consumers to deploy their subjectivity in defining the character of goods for themselves, and they are not necessarily innocent and compliant victims of advertisers in this respect. Consumers reflect upon and, if insisting on using the terminology, *make* their own utility functions through inner speculation on the meaning of goods to themselves. Otherwise, there is literally nothing to distinguish the human consumer from any other non-human consumer, animal or even machine, for the consumer is little more than a mini-factory for producing utility (see below on the affinity between producer and consumer theory). Indeed, debates about the relationship between false and real needs, the role of hidden persuaders, and whether consumer sovereignty over the economy genuinely prevails are notable for their absence from consumer theory within mainstream economics.

Third, this opens up the significance of *external* influences on the individual's more broadly interpreted subjectivity. Consumption is based upon social factors such as emulation and distinction (much emphasised in the sociology of consumption), and upon cultures, norms and ethnographies of consumption more generally (much emphasised in the anthropology of consumption). At least in part, individual subjectivity is surely influenced, if not primarily determined, by social norms.

Fourth, it is not simply the motivation and influences upon the consumer that are so narrowly conceived within the mainstream but also the notion of consumption itself. As is often recognised terminologically by neoclassical economics, consumer theory is no such thing. Rather, whatever its merits, it is *demand* theory alone. It merely purports to offer a quantitative analysis of how much of a good will be demanded in what is a static exercise in optimisation. The range of activities associated with the attachment of demand to consumption is overlooked, in reducing consumption to the moment of purchase alone. But the acts of purchase (from anticipation to shopping) through to use and, ultimately, disposal all form integral elements in consumption and interact with individual subjectivity and its determinants in complex and varying ways. This is readily captured in popular parlance – 'a house is not a home'; 'you are what you eat'; 'dedicated followers of fashion'; let alone 'no logo' – which appeals to a lifestyle that eschews lifestyle by branding whilst, at the same time, emphasising how important branding is.

So far, emphasis has been placed on how heavily stripped down, almost to the point of non-existence, the consumer of neoclassical theory is. This is an individual torn from time, place and context, and from speculative and socially conditioned behaviour. All that needs to be known is a utility function, from which can be determined demand for each and every good depending upon prices, income and possibly other constraints. But, as is already implicit, by the same token there is an equally parsimonious treatment of the *goods* that make up the consumer's object of desire (itself surely a richer concept than utility). Significantly, and literally, goods are denoted by symbols, $x_1, x_2, x_3, \ldots,$ x_n. They have no distinguishing features other than their subscript index, and this is only so that they can be allocated a corresponding price and position in the individual's utility function (rather than in the home, on the plate, on the body, in the driveway, etc.). This conforms neatly with the parallel reduced understanding of the consumer as (human) individual. If the latter were able genuinely to be subjective and to be subject to social influences in consumer behaviour (including but over and above demand), so consumer goods would have properties over and above what is presumably their physical characteristics, however well the latter might be defined and known to the consumer. In particular, goods would have meanings attached to them by consumers, and these meanings would depend upon both inner reflection and (in interaction with) social determinants.

As a result, it is hardly surprising that a (if not the) major aspect of advertising is designed not to convey *information* about goods but to suggest the meanings that might be attached to those goods both to the consumer and to others who witness consumption – the consumer looking at others looking at the consumer. This can be careful and subtle, as well as crude and bombastic – appealing to the consumer as super-normal (happy families) or as super-abnormal (as goods attached to or to endow the impossible).

The point here is not to assess whether and how such advertising works. Rather, the practice of advertising is indicative of a wider, arguably more important, set of considerations that influence consumption and the consumer. These are precluded by neoclassical consumer theory by virtue of its limited understanding of the individual, the social, and the corresponding nature of both the consumer and the consumed. Indeed, the *presence* of such factors are so pervasive from our own individual experience as consumers (if not as trained economists) that it becomes a mystery how the neoclassical theory of the consumer should take their *exclusion* as its conventional starting point. It should be emphasised that this exclusion is not an oversight but is built into the foundations of the theory – fixed preferences, single (utility maximising) motivation, and individuals and goods that are treated so abstractly and generally that they are without identity and meaning, respectively. How did this (and worse, as will be seen) come about?

2.3 How Consumer Theory Got its Spots

As suggested in Chapter 1, during the course of the nineteenth century the idea of economic rationality came to the fore, corresponding to the view that the spread of markets (and capitalism) had created a distinct sphere of economic activity in which self-interest would be predominantly if not exclusively pursued. Wedded with utilitarianism that had also gathered strength at the same time, this all came together through the marginalist revolution of the 1870s to distil the consumer as a utility-maximising individual pursuing self-interest through the market. As already mentioned, not much has been added to this under-standing of the consumer other than technical detail. But, in this case, the devil has been in the detail, or at least has been inspired by it.

Indeed, focus on detail has been crucial to the growing and unquestioned acceptance of consumer theory as it is today. From the 1870s to the 1950s, the task that the marginalists set themselves was to place its consumer theory on as secure a footing as possible. Here 'secure' refers to formal technical details as opposed to more informal presentations in terms of marginal utilities and prices. As a result, what drove consumer theory in this period was the making of assumptions and the adoption of methods and meanings in pursuit of the derivation of technical results more or less irrespective of other considerations, including realism – and, it might be added, common experience let alone sense.

In short, the goal was to obtain well-defined demand curves on the basis of utility-maximising individuals and to establish the properties of such demand curves. Some of the preconditions for this have already been highlighted. Others can now be added at a greater level of detail. First, consider the notion of utility itself. Even today, outside of economics, it is associated (as with the philosophy of utilitarianism) with general well-being however determined. But, within the economics of consumer behaviour, utility has been reduced to the simple satisfaction derived hedonistically from the consumption of goods. This is in order that the theory can become a matter or logic of choice between one available bundle of goods and another without reference to other considera-tions. In short, the shift from utility to utility function is a heavy reduction of analytical and conceptual content that, despite the distance between the two, is simply disregarded in consumer theory.

Second, certain technical assumptions are necessary for utility maximisation to work satisfactorily. These include 'continuity' and 'convexity' of preferences in the technical jargon (and there are other requirements including transitivity of preferences). These are necessary to ensure that the more familiar indifference curves are appropriately shaped so that a budget line defines a maximum with correspondingly appropriate equality between relative marginal utilities and relative prices (Diagram 2.1). The presumption is, for example, that consumption of mixtures of goods is superior to concentrated consumption of a few goods. This might be justified on the grounds that variety is the spice of life, but even when it comes to working with spices this nostrum surely fails as does a non-satiation condition – that more consumption without limit always gives higher utility. The important point is that the conditions or assumptions necessary to make neoclassical consumer theory work are entirely arbitrary from the point of view of consumption itself – at one level it is an empirical matter that can and will go either way. The assumptions depend upon totally unwarranted and unjustifiable generalisations from particular examples or principles. The assumptions are only made because they are needed for the theory to work.

Significantly, usually little attempt is made to justify the assumptions, with presentation devoted to elaborating the technical details and implications of the assumptions as opposed to their correspondence to consumption in practice. It has to be suspected that if the opposite assumptions had been necessary for

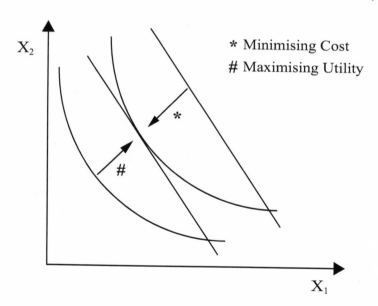

Diagram 2.1   Is this an isoquant or an indifference curve?

the theory to work, these assumptions would have been made instead. Indeed, this is exactly and more generally what economists do in making assumptions within their deductive methodology. Assumptions are made for the convenience of the theory not in light of the object of study. You will find that real-world examples used in textbooks to illustrate the principles by reference to particular goods, such as chalk and cheese, are no such thing. These specific goods are used, if at all rather than x_1 and x_2, as illustrative devices not as illustrations. Nothing is learned about chalk and cheese as such, let alone the more appropriately abstract widgets.

These technical assumptions underpinning consumer theory seem outrageous until they become second nature to the practising economist. Third, though, the acceptance of these principles was also dependent upon profound shifts in the nature of economics as a discipline. On the one hand, it became detached from other disciplines, especially those dealing with consumption from other perspectives such as sociology, psychology, history and anthropology. This is associated with economics becoming reduced to a particular version of the science of the market – that seeking purely to explain the logic of supply and demand. On the other hand, economics experienced a shift in, and narrowing of, method. The economic rationality of the optimising individual serves as the basic building block; and the theory depends upon axiomatic deduction from assumptions about individuals that have no basis in empirical investigation.

Not surprisingly, neither the progress in establishing the technical results nor the acceptance of their significance was achieved immediately. Significantly, during the interwar period, such microeconomics, as it was to become when complemented with the corresponding theory of the firm and supply, was primarily perceived as relevant to at most one part of economic behaviour and analysis: precisely that concerned with the isolated, optimising individual. This detached it not only from other social sciences but also from other branches of economics, especially those concerned with the systemic functioning of the economy as a whole. As a result, the explicit distinction between microeconomics and macroeconomics first emerged in the 1930s, with the presumption that (Keynesian) macroeconomics would address the major problems of the day for which marginalist principles were at most of marginal use. In addition, other inductive traditions were strong in economics at this time, especially institutional economics (itself particularly influential in the United States) for which attention to social organisation and processes of the economy in practice took precedence over abstract deductive principles, particularly those focused on the optimising individual.

However, in the decade following the Second World War, the situation within economics as a discipline changed dramatically. First, the technical apparatus around consumer theory had essentially already been developed as fully as it could be. Given that a consumer has a utility function and maximises that utility subject to given prices and budget constraints, what are the consequences for the properties of the derived demand curves? Putting this issue the other way, suppose there is a wish to posit demand curves for theoretical purposes and/ or empirical estimation: what restrictions must be placed on what form these curves take? It might be expected that they would be positive, for example in own price (although if prices of certain goods became really high, consumers might start to supply rather than to demand them). This is a straightforward enough question but getting hold of the answer was not so simple. As students of elementary economics know, demand for a good is not only dependent upon its own price but also potentially on the price of all other goods. As a result, demand curves may not be downward sloping in own price, as classically drawn in the diagram of supply and demand curves crossing one another. The higher price implies lower real income overall as lesser bundles of goods can be purchased with the same money income. So it is possible that utility will be maximised for a higher price on an 'inferior' good by consuming more and not less of that good despite its increase in price.

This is not difficult to understand. Suppose a consumer wishes to meet certain dietary requirements but prefers to do so, if income allows, by moving up the scale of more expensive (presumably higher quality) foods. If the price of basic foods increases, it may be necessary to consume more and not less of these to meet dietary needs. Again, as is well known, such inferior goods have a negative income effect (other things being equal, demand decreases as income increases). If that negative income effect is sufficiently large, it can outweigh the substitution effect of consuming less of goods purely because of their increase in price, once correcting for the corresponding loss of income. If the demand for a good increases when its price increases, it is known as a Giffen good.

This is all standard stuff in demand theory, so much so that you can readily find it on Wikipedia[1] and Diagram 2.2. It follows that there is no simple relationship between changing prices and changing patterns of demand even with the heroic assumptions made around fixed, continuous and convex preferences. What has been achieved with consumer theory is to explore these conundrums fully and to find what properties must be satisfied for demand curves to be truly representative of the underlying optimising behaviour of an individual. One property, for example, akin to the absence of money illusion, is that demand should be homogeneous of degree zero in income and prices. In less technical terms, if all prices and income are doubled (or changed by the same factor), then demand should remain the same. In other words, it should make no difference to demand if prices and incomes are calculated in pennies rather than pounds or dollars.

1. http://en.wikipedia.org/wiki/Inferior_good (accessed December 2015).

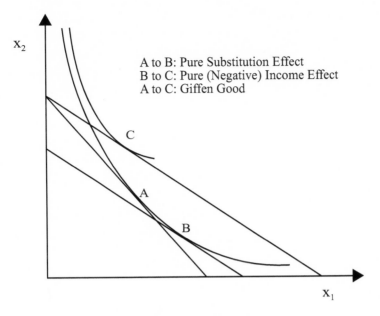

A to B: Pure Substitution Effect
B to C: Pure (Negative) Income Effect
A to C: Giffen Good

Diagram 2.2   Giffen good

Further – and this was the major discovery for consumer theory – demand curves should be negative in own price and positive in the price of other goods if income is adjusted for those price changes so that the level of utility remains the same. In technical terms, with movement around an indifference curve, there is substitution of the relatively cheaper other goods for less of the more expensive. This property is important in defining the necessary and sufficient conditions for specified demand curves to have been derived from optimising behaviour.

For completeness, this can be expressed formally for the reader who wishes and is able to follow it through. Suppose the standard utility function $u(x_1, ..., x_n)$ is used. Recall that this is supposed to be underpinned by a set of preferences out of which the utility function, u, is derived. With prices p_i and income I, then maximise u subject to $p_1x_1 + ... + p_nx_n = I$, the budget constraint. Solving this problem gives what are called the Marshallian, direct, observed or uncompensated demand curves for each of the goods, $x_i = g_i(p_1, ..., p_n, I)$. The terms direct, observed and uncompensated are all used in order to indicate that these functions, under the assumptions made, represent the demand that would be directly observed at these prices and income without compensating for any loss (or gain) of income in light of what the prices are in order to keep the level of utility constant.

By substituting these demand curves back into the utility function, there will be obtained a complicated function out of the u and the g_is, namely $u(g_1(p_1, ..., p_n, I), ..., g_i(p_1, ..., p_n, I), ..., g_n(p_1, ..., p_n, I))$. This can be simply rewritten as a function of the prices and income alone, without reference to the derived g_i, and is known as the indirect utility function $v(p_1, ..., p_n, I)$. This is the solution to the maximising problem as it reveals, given u, how much utility can be derived by the optimising individual when facing prices p_i and income I. v is known as the indirect utility function because, although it tells how much utility can be achieved, it is a function of prices and incomes that allow for that utility rather than the goods bought and consumed in getting it. So v does not give utility directly – that only comes from the goods x_i – but v does indicate how much utility can be gained at given prices and income (for the initial utility function, u).

It is relatively easy to show that g_i and v are all homogeneous of degree 0 in prices and income (double these and demands remain the same as does the maximum utility that can be obtained). So, given a utility function with the right properties, the demand problem can be solved. But what about the other way around? If someone offered a set of demand curves, $g_i(p_1, ..., p_n, I)$, or the indirect utility function v, could these be worked backwards to discover the utility function, u, from which they were derived? The answer is a *qualified* yes. If starting with v instead of u, the Marshallian demand curves can be obtained. This is as a result of what is known as Roy's identity, stated here without proof and which shows that $g_i(p_1, ..., p_n, I) = -(\delta v/\delta p_i)/(\delta v/\delta I)$.[2] In other words, given v, there is a route back to the g_i. With minor qualification, it is also possible to go back from the g_i to get the utility function u.[3] This means that the journey can now effectively be taken back to v by using the g_i and the u derived from them.

---

2.   This can be interpreted as follows. As the consumer is already optimising, the major (first order) effect of increasing a price on the utility you can get is equivalent to the extra income needed to buy what you were already buying (and substituting into other goods is of second order importance).

3.   It is known, subject to continuity, that it is possible to go from preferences to a utility function u but there is not a one-to-one correspondence between the preferences and the utility function. This is because any monotonic transformation of u also represents the same preferences. This is equivalent to having the same indifference curves (these do represent the preferences uniquely) but labelling each of them with a different number. The order of the indifference curves is all that is needed, not the quantity of utility that is assigned to them. For this reason, utility as defined by indifference curves is known as ordinal. In a sense, it is like temperature – it can be known what is more or less (hotter or colder) but it is arbitrary how this is graded. This means that it is not possible to go back from the Marshallian demand curves (or indirect utility function) to a unique utility function, u. All that can be done is to get back to a utility function subject to monotonic transformation (although this does represent the preferences uniquely). To do this, from the Marshallian demand curves, start with the n equations, $x_i = g_i(p_1, ..., p_n, I)$, take one price, p_1 say, as numeraire or set equal to 1, and solve for I as a function of the x_i. This can serve as a utility function as utility increases with income, I, but any monotonic transformation of the function I would serve equally well as a utility function and give us the same Marshallian demand curves. But the indirect utility function, v, would be different depending on what utility function is used to represent preferences.

What has been shown is that, with minor qualification, preferences, utility function, Marshallian demand functions and indirect utility function are all equivalent to one another in terms of the information they contain. This is useful but, as it stands, it still does not indicate what properties are needed to be imposed on the Marshallian demand functions or the indirect utility function to guarantee that they are derived from an optimising individual with a given utility function, u say. Because of inferior good type problems, it cannot even be presumed that the direct demand functions are negative in own price. But now consider what is termed the dual problem of minimising the income that you need in order to obtain a given level of utility, u say. This is the same problem as before but the other way round. The goal is to get to a given indifference curve by using the least amount of income as opposed to getting to the highest indifference curve by using a given amount of income (Diagram 2.1). Graphically, both problems are represented by tangency between indifference curve and budget line, whichever one is being moved about as opposed to the other being fixed. This means they are essentially the same problem which is why they are given the name of primal and dual, depending on which one you start with, and there is a fixed correspondence between the solutions involved.

For the dual, minimise $I = p_1 x_1 + \ldots + p_n x_n$ subject to $u(x_1, \ldots, x_n) = u$, that is, the problem is to find the consumption bundle, the x_i, for given prices, p_i, that gives the minimum cost, I, of achieving a given level of utility, u, (rather than maximising utility for a given amount to spend). When this problem is solved, the result is what is termed the Hicksian (the opposite or dual of the Marshallian), indirect, unobserved, compensated demand curves. They are indirect in the sense that consumers have no idea as such of a level of utility that they are seeking to realise. By the same token, they are unobserved as consumers go about making expenditures on the basis of income and prices, not on unobserved utility targets. And they are compensated in the sense that, whatever happens to prices, the consumer is given just enough income to get to a pre-assigned level of utility.

Represent Hicksian demand curves by $h_i(p_1, \ldots, p_n, u)$, the amount of good x_i that will be bought given these prices and the need to get to utility, u, using minimum income. Adding up $p_1 h_1 + \ldots + p_i h_i \ldots + p_n h_n$ gives the solution to the problem and the corresponding expenditure or cost function $I = I(p_1, \ldots, p_n, u)$, the amount of income needed to get utility u when prices are p_i. This, then, is the minimum cost of getting utility u given prices p_i. Suppose, though, that the expenditure function, I, is offered as the starting point. Is it possible to get back to the Hicksian demand functions and the underlying utility function? Once again, the answer is yes. By a result known as Shephard's lemma,[4] it is possible

---

4. Given the individual is already optimising, the extra income needed to get a given level of utility in response to a price increase is to buy what was being bought already, with substitution possibilities of a second order effect.

to retrieve the Hicksian demand functions from the expenditure function, since $\delta I(p_1, ..., p_n, u)/\delta p_i = h_i(p_1, ..., p_n, u)$. It is also possible to retrieve the utility function from the Hicksian demand functions.[5]

In addition, the functions I and v are essentially the same as one another. They are inverses – one taking income as the dependent variable, the other taking utility as the dependent variable. So writing $I = I(p_1, ..., p_n, u)$ is the same thing as writing $u = v(p_1, ..., p_n, I)$. It is a bit of a mouthful but this can be put into words. What utility could be gained with income I at given prices, if I is the minimum amount of income that is needed to get that level of utility, u? The answer is u. And what income is needed to get utility u at given prices, p_i, if u is the utility gained with income I at those prices? The answer is I. In symbols, the following are identities (they must be true), respectively, $u = v(p_1, ..., p_n, I(p_1, ..., p_n, u))$ and $I = I(p_1, ..., p_n, v(p_1, ..., p_n, I))$.

This means that there is a strict correspondence between the Marshallian indirect utility function and the Hicksian expenditure function. One is equivalent to the other and one can be obtained from the other by rearranging what is set equal to what: u as a function of prices and income, or income as a function of price and utility. But, as already demonstrated, the different steps along the Marshallian system are all equivalent to one another, from preferences to indirect utility function and back again, subject to monotonicity of the utility function, so the same applies across these and all the steps in the Hicksian dual demand system.

This is all illustrated in Diagram 2.3, and it is a satisfying and elegant representation of the correspondence between different ways of approaching the consumer (as utility maximiser given prices and income or as expenditure minimiser given need to attain a given level of utility at given prices). But it goes much further than this, once the properties of the Hicksian demand functions are explored. It is now possible to tease out exactly what the required properties of the demand system are (one that is obtained from an optimising consumer). There are some obvious and readily identifiable properties. For example, the Hicksian demand functions (and expenditure function) should be homogeneous of degree one in prices – if all prices are doubled, exactly the same will be bought as before, with relative marginal utilities equalling relative marginal prices, but twice the income will be needed to do it. As already indicated, though, the main problem is that associated with inferior goods and with the interaction between substitution and, potentially perversely outweighing, income effects. The beauty of the Hicksian system is that it eliminates the income effect by compensating

5. From $x_i = h_i(p_1, ..., p_n, u)$, there are n equations in the prices $p_1, ..., p_n$, the quantities $x_1, ..., x_n$, and u. But the hi are homogeneous of degree zero (you buy the same consumption bundle if all prices double to get a given quantity of utility, it will just cost you double). This means p_1, say, can be set equal to unity, and eliminate the p_i from the n equations to get u as a function of the x_i. This is to retrieve the original utility function, u.

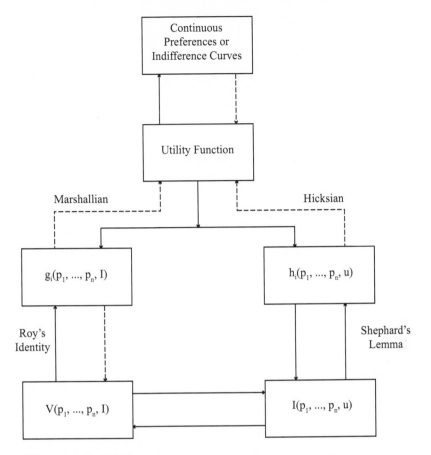

All boxes are equivalent
Those connected by dashed lines are subject to monotonicity

Diagram 2.3   The complete and closed system of neoclassical consumer theory

for it with constant utility. This means that its properties are well defined (by analogy with moving round an indifference curve in response to relative price changes in the budget line). Doing this always means consuming less of goods with higher prices and more of goods with the same prices, the pure substitution effect that the Hicksian system is designed to capture, as in moving the budget line around the indifference curve in Diagram 2.1.

In formal terms, this can all be derived from the mathematical properties of the Hicksian expenditure function, I. As already known, from Shephard's lemma, $h_i = \delta I / \delta p_i$. Further, then, because of the pure substitution effect, $\delta h_i / \delta p_j$ should be positive unless $i = j$, in which case it is negative (own price effect as demand goes down with increased price in absence of income effect). In addition, because the order of differentiation does not make any difference to outcome, $\delta^2 I / \delta p_i \delta p_j =$

$\delta h_j/\delta p_i = \delta h_i/\delta p_j = \delta^2 I/\delta p_j \delta p_i$, and these are all positive unless $i = j$ for which they are negative. In other words, substituting along an indifference curve from one good i to another good j is equal and opposite to going the other way round, and is positive (in the constructed absence of income effects as there is no hopping between indifference curves).

Now it turns out that (alongside homogeneity, etc., already discussed) these properties of the Hicksian demand functions are just necessary and sufficient for them to have been derived from the optimising behaviour of the individual.[6] This means that it is possible to work with the Hicksian demand system for theoretical problems, and use the mathematical properties of the system for the purposes of comparative statics (the properties of a new equilibrium in case of a change in the tax system, for example). Also a proposed Marshallian demand system can be taken, transformed into its Hicksian counterpart, and checked that it satisfies the necessary and sufficient conditions for being derived from optimising behaviour. In that way, when empirically estimating the Marshallian system from observed data, there can be an assurance that properly constituted demand curves are being deployed. Alternatively, a Hicksian demand system can be taken and translated into a Marshallian system for estimation.

2.4 Consumer Theory Hoist by its Own Petard

In short, on its own terms, this consumer theory is satisfyingly complete – allowing it to be both well founded in terms of squeezing out all there is from the assumption of optimising behaviour. This, in turn, provides for theoretical and empirical work to be carried out with corresponding implications for policy. It is a remarkable achievement and can hardly be improved upon – once accepting its severe limitations. Possibly the reader, like the pioneering theorists themselves, has been carried along by the technical imperatives and the corresponding chase to pin down the properties of demand curves despite the problems posed by perverse income effects. But what has come out is neither more nor less than what has gone in. And, as is apparent from the presentation, the only input to this exercise is the consumer's set of given preferences and the presumption of utility maximisation (top of Diagram 2.3).

This is obviously extremely limited in analytical content and application, as will be demonstrated by two issues. The first concerns the notion that demand can, for what is called a Giffen good, go up with price because of its inferior quality. But it has also been established that demand for a good can go up with its price for entirely different *reasons* and for entirely different *goods*:

---

6.   It is equivalent to requiring that the matrix with typical element $\delta^2 I/\delta p_i \delta p_j$ should be symmetric, have positive elements off the diagonal and negative elements on the diagonal. These also guarantee that a minimum income is being obtained from the optimising for the dual.

those associated with luxury. This is as a result of what is called the Veblen effect, with Thorstein Veblen strongly associated with the idea of conspicuous consumption. If a luxury good goes up in price, it becomes strongly associated with esteem and as a symbol of status and wealth. The same can apply as a motive for consumption irrespective of price changes, as sociologists have recognised in terms of emulation and distinction underpinning consumer behaviour (keeping up with, or staying ahead of, the Joneses). So this is not just a matter of elite or luxury consumption, as is also apparent from consumption choices over branded and own-label goods, with one liable but not guaranteed to offer greater consumer satisfaction simply because of its image of higher quality – something deliberately targeted by advertisements. It follows that dividing changes in demand between income and substitution effects, even for the individual consumer, is liable mistakenly to overlook both other influences on consumer behaviour associated with interdependent, not given, preferences across consumers, and motives other than utility maximisation. As is apparent from even this brief discussion, to which goods these considerations might apply is likely neither to be uniform across goods, across time nor across consumers. The theory might be prepared, in empirical application, to assign what it does not explain statistically as being due to shifts in preferences. But those shifts in preferences that reinforce those associated with shifts in prices and incomes will be counted as income and substitution effects.

This all arises because of the exclusion of so many of the determinants of consumer behaviour, and the difficulty of accommodating them even if the attempt were made. Did the taste for chicken rise because of the reduction in its price or because of a shift in tastes towards chicken? A second problem is one within the theory and, to some extent, of its own making. This is how to deploy the theory of a single consumer to explore demand as a whole: the aggregation problem. Put more precisely, if a demand function for the economy as a whole is to be estimated, just drawing upon the economy's overall income and the price system, is it legitimate to use the demand system derived for an individual? In other words, can demand functions be estimated independently of the distribution of income and preferences across consumers?

Not surprisingly, the answer is no in general, and the conditions for it to be yes are extremely stringent, indeed unrealistically so. Essentially, the economy as a whole needs to consume as if it were a single individual with a given income. But if taking income from one consumer and giving it to another, the pattern of demand will be different unless those two consumers have matching preferences as far as demand is concerned. So it is necessary to assume that each and every consumer has suitably similar preferences. However, even this assumption is not enough. Suppose it is true, and take income from a rich person and give it to a poor person. Their patterns of consumption around their initial levels of income are liable to be very different: luxuries as opposed to necessities. So, redistributing the income from rich to poor will not leave demand unchanged but shift it from luxuries to necessities. To have an aggregate demand function as if the economy were a single individual it is necessary *both* that all individuals have the same preferences as one another *and* that those preferences remain in the same proportions at every level of income (or, to put it another way, once you know just one indifference curve for the representative individual, you know them all, not only for that consumer but for all others as well – all consumers must have the same, so-called homothetic indifference curves). To be sure that the aggregation problem can be negotiated, it is necessary that the economy's demand be reduced to a *single* indifference curve. Relative prices indicate where consumption is on the curve in relative proportions, and aggregate income tells us how much is consumed. Otherwise, it matters which individuals get which level of income to spend. Significantly, the insurmountable nature of the aggregation problem is well established within the orthodoxy, as a result of what is known as the Sonnenschein–Mantel–Debreu theorem but, as with so much else that is uncomfortable for the mainstream, it is most observed in the breach.

Obviously this is entirely unacceptable, but it is in part a consequence of the failure to take account of both income distribution as a factor in demand and that preferences are not independent of one another. This is all at least implicitly recognised in empirical work in practice by estimating different demand functions for different sections of the population: by age, gender, region, class, household type, etc. With enhanced and cheapened computer power, this has become more common, even commonplace, as a consequence of the more readily available data sets at household level and the capacity to undertake sophisticated econometrics with these data. But there is a paradox here. For the theory takes preferences as given as the basis on which to construct its theory of consumer behaviour. Yet, in order to implement the theory empirically, it is explicitly accepted that certain variables are systematic sources of differences in, or identity of, preferences. Surely the theory should investigate what these are and why?

2.5 Consumer Theory as Economics Imperialism

So far, the dynamic and imperative of consumer theory have been highlighted, together with its most immediate results and consequences. A narrowly defined, but challenging, problem was eventually solved by an extraordinary reduction of the nature of how consumer theory came to be constructed, with an implosion of the scope of the analysis so that it only included fixed preferences, over fixed goods, and subject to utility maximisation alone. To some extent, the elegance as well as the completeness of the solution offered some rationale for it to become a core component of mainstream microeconomics. It also had the advantage of being able to be presented at different levels of complexity and sophistication – from the informal notion of equality of ratios of marginal utilities to relative prices through indifference curves, utility functions, and income and substitution effects in diagrams to the duality between Marshallian and Hicksian systems of demand.

But the place and influence of consumer theory within an evolving mainstream neoclassical economics extends beyond its immediate object of analysis. First and foremost, once complemented by producer theory, and aggregating over all economic agents, consumer theory has served as a major element in establishing general equilibrium theory as the central accomplishment of microeconomics. Married to producer theory, consumer theory offered an understanding of the workings of the economy as a whole, drawing upon the optimising behaviour of individuals whether in supply or demand. Such general equilibrium theory was essentially established in its modern form in the 1950s at much the same time that consumer theory had formally ironed out its own difficulties. In short, the consumer theory of demand is an essential component and leading illustration of the centrality of the technical apparatus and technical architecture of micro-economics (TA^2) discussed in Chapter 1.

Second, this also paved the way for the formalist revolution in economics, with the increasing reliance upon mathematical methods and deductive modelling as the form taken by economic theory. Whilst the use of mathematics in mainstream economics is now taken for granted, this is not just a matter of style of argument but also reflects a profound shift in the content of the economics as well. Certainly, the use of mathematics in economics is independent in principle to a large degree from its substantive content. But consumer and producer theory (and general equilibrium theory) as core topics within economics promoted the use of mathematics, and the use of mathematics returned the favour. Nor, as previously mentioned, was the formalisation confined to microeconomics. Keynesian macroeconomics, without relying upon such microeconomics, was also increasingly presented, however faithfully, in mathematical terms, especially with the use of the IS/LM framework as the standard textbook treatment.

Third, nor did this formalist revolution take place in an intellectual, political and ideological vacuum. It was heavily associated with the rapid expansion of teaching and research in economics in the United States. The Americanisation of economics involved a significant and rapid shift of the centre of gravity for the discipline from the UK to the US. It was also associated with the 'professionalisation' of the discipline, and standardised textbooks around standardised material, with the exclusion of other considerations from within economics itself (increasingly marginalised as heterodox) and from other disciplines. During the time of the formalist revolution, the Cold War and anti-communism were at their height. Those promoting Keynesianism, despite its impeccable intellectual and political origins in the mission to save capitalism from itself through prevention of crises of deficient effective (possibly consumer) demand, ran the risk of being dubbed as communists.

It is important neither to exaggerate nor to distort the intellectual and ideological thrust underpinning the formalist revolution. It certainly was not inspired by anti-communism and neoliberalism. Yet it was entirely compatible with these, not least for those adopting an extreme position in hostility to state intervention and advising of the benefits of the market. This is apparent in the idea of consumer sovereignty and what have been called the fundamental theorems of welfare economics. Left to its own devices, the market serves the consumer, all of us, and no one can be made better off without someone else being made worse off. Equally, though, the formalist revolution was compatible with emphasis on market imperfections at both macro and micro levels, in light of deficiency of effective demand and the presence of externalities and monopoly. But the way in which the imperfectly working market could be conceived within economics was heavily constrained by its dependence upon the newly established core principles. This is true analytically, other than in Keynesian macroeconomics with its emphasis on systemic deficient demand, in the sense of still relying upon optimising individuals with given utility functions, etc., and with a corresponding neglect of, and lack of contact with, the approaches of the other social sciences concerned with power, conflict, institutions and so on. It was also true ideologically given that market imperfections were to be perceived as something that could be corrected within capitalism, usually by a benevolent state, or by the formation of other institutions.

Nonetheless, with economics imperialism, even consumer theory has been enabled to bring back in those factors that had been left out, even if to a minimal extent. This is because the utility function as part of the TA^2 is particularly vulnerable to any deviations from its requirements, especially those conceptually grounded in given individuals and goods, that is, the utility function itself. Begin to vary these in any fashion and the whole apparatus of optimisation tends to collapse. So, the BBI tends to be confined to supplementing utility functions and optimising behaviour with added factors. This might be focused on the individual, the social or somewhere in between. Individuals might, for example, choose to be altruistic whether in pursuit of their own interests to overcome collective action problems or genuinely as a variable in their utility function to be chosen like apples and pears (whether at a cost or for mutual gain).

The result is what might be termed mixed or dirty models. Whether for theoretical or empirical expediency, the standard technical apparatus is augmented by some other factor or set of factors appropriated from another social science or simply through speculative reasoning, especially with various propositions from behavioural economics. This is to bridge the previous divide between rational and irrational. A good example is the recently prominent economics of happiness where populations do not seem to report themselves happier despite rising incomes over time. It is a simple matter to add some other variable to utility theory in order to address this, the most convenient being reference to relative income position. Then it becomes possible to explain why short-run increases in one person's income improves feelings of well-being, but the same is not true for improvements in income for everybody over time as relative positions remain the same.

This is, however, to open a can of worms as far as utility theory is concerned. If utility is not given exogenously by the set of preferences attached to an individual but is subject to (social) influences, through comparison with others for example, then it is far from clear why other social influences should not be brought to bear. And these might have entirely different effects across different consumption goods. It is entirely arbitrary, or at least historically accidental, to start modifying given utility functions in order to explain why they are not given, and to incorporate factors that were previously excluded in order to allow utility functions to prevail in the first place.

In this way, it can be seen that within economics and across the social sciences more generally, it has become commonplace to deploy the notion of the utility-maximising consumer (and other elements of neoclassical economics) to address any number of problems, even those apparently unrelated to (market) consumption as such. A recent example is provided by the economics of identity, understood as an element in a utility function (giving more or less utility depending upon the identities chosen by others). Significantly, this has been pioneered by George Akerlof, a leading exponent and Nobel Prize winner for the market and information imperfections approach to economics. Thus, whilst this has promoted the new phase of economics imperialism as an apparent reaction against the old-style and neoliberal notion that markets work well, the effect has been to consolidate and extend the status of the utility function for the study of consumption as well as for much else besides. Paradoxically, considerations of identity should lead to the rejection of the utility function as the basis for understanding consumption. Instead, identity is treated as if it were (a flawed) element of consumption within a given utility function. But what are the alternatives?

2.6 From Consumer Theory to Systems of Provision

The weaknesses of the neoclassical theory of consumption derive from what was necessary to get it established, and which persisted to a large extent once it had been established. They can be summarised as: the limited motivation and capacities of individual consumers; the reduction of consumption to the limited act of purchase as opposed to the processes attached to consumption from anticipation through to disposal, quite apart from supply of goods themselves; the failure to specify the nature of consumption goods themselves,

as well as of individuals, other than in the most abstract fashion; the failure
to take account of social influences and context; failure to recognise that the
nature of consumption goods and of individuals depends upon time, place and
circumstance, and in interdependence with other individuals as individuals and
as members of social categories defined by gender, class, race, nationality, etc.;
an exaggerated dependence upon axiomatic, deductive methods focused upon
individual optimisation despite the limited empirical applicability of theoretical
results in light of aggregation problems; and a failure to engage with the insights
of other social sciences, not least as these have been heavily preoccupied with
consumption across an extremely wide range of considerations that have been
studiously ignored by economics.

The final point is true in many different ways. Not surprisingly, given the
importance of consumption and demand to the profitability of commercial
enterprise, consumer theory (especially when attached to marketing science)
has focused upon the motivation and behaviour of consumers and the meaning
of goods to them, with some attention to the role played by advertising. Such
studies have ranged over the psychology of consumers as well as the various
variables associated with socio-demographics, sorting consumers into varieties
of lifestyles that may or may not induce, or associate them with, common
purchasing patterns. From such approaches alone, a hundred or more variables
can readily be teased out as influences upon consumption, with much emphasis
upon empirical relevance as opposed to theoretical depth – although socio-psy-
chological theories are in abundance.

On the other hand, traditional treatments of consumption across other
disciplines have been more analytical in content. For sociology, there is the idea
of common patterns or norms of consumption that are socially determined.
These may be complemented by social processes internalised by individuals,
such as emulation, distinction and conspicuous consumption. Perhaps it is
significant that the latter is most closely associated with Veblen, usually thought
of as an economist, even though his theory of the consequential possibility of
increasing demand as price increases would undermine standard theory. For
anthropology, the significance of consumption is to be found in the different
meanings that are associated with the consumed and the consumer, in extreme
form when it comes to taboo, display or festival, religious or otherwise. It is
obvious, but absented from neoclassical theory, that much of the meaning
attached to consumption, and hence demand for consumer goods, must be
socially determined and not simply derived from the physical properties of
those goods. This became such a preoccupation of consumer theory outside
of economics at the height of postmodernism that the symbolic meaning of
consumer goods took precedence over, even to the point of excluding, the
material content of those goods. Not so much as the victims of advertising, but

more out of their own volition, consumers could imagine consumption to be whatever they wanted, and to symbolise this to self and potentially to others.

For the purposes of offering an alternative approach to consumption, the problem is less one of recognising this wider set of determinants than in placing them within an appropriate analytical framework. Within different social science disciplines, there has been a tendency to put forward what has been termed horizontal theories. The classic example is economics itself with its dependence upon utility theory. This is horizontal in the sense that the theory applies across all consumption goods, and even determines the consumption of each good simultaneously, without regard to the differences between the goods other than by virtue of some notional differences in price and physical properties. But much the same can be said of many contributions from other disciplines, in the sense that emulation and distinction, for example, or conspicuous consumption, could apply to each and every good in principle. Psychological motives for consumption are also presumed to apply in principle to each and every good, across all of them. The goods only enter after the event in terms of whether they can or cannot, or do or do not empirically, meet the theoretically prior properties required of them.

On this basis, it might be thought that the best way to proceed is to stack together all the horizontal theories to be found and furnish a more or less complete theory of consumption. This will not work, though, because these theories will tend to be mutually incompatible, and there is no guarantee that all of the relevant factors will have been gathered together nor combined and distributed appropriately across particular items of consumption. An alternative is to reject the idea that there can be a general theory of consumption at all, from which individual elements of consumption can be addressed. And, in place of a horizontal approach, a vertical approach can be adopted, one that focuses upon particular items of consumption. Then, for these, it is a matter of examining how consumption is tied to its determinants, both materially and culturally. This will vary from commodity to commodity. But it is possible to trace how each of housing, food, clothing, transport, entertainment, etc., is attached to a different mode or system of provision, running from production to consumption, including the formation of corresponding norms and cultures (levels and meanings) of consumption. Second, such norms are not to be perceived as a single standard across everybody nor as an average level of consumption with some above or below to reflect these differences in consumption across and within commodities. Rather, the consumption of each commodity will vary across the population in terms of levels, modes and meanings of consumption. From an empirical point of view, the task is first and foremost to *identify* these norms of consumption as socially determined by socio-economic variables such as class, gender, age, race and region. Then these must be explained. In contrast, neoclassical consumer theory starts with the individual, constructs a theory, and then estimates empirical outcomes as an explanation rather than as something to be explained.

Thus, in the case of clothing for example, it would be necessary to examine the fashion system and how it is connected to the production of clothing (across everything from high-class design to sweated child labour), its distribution and sale, and its display in the acts of consumption itself, with very different outcomes and determinants across countries, gender, class, etc. This is not to say that price and income are not important – far from it, as much of the fashion system is about segmented markets and the shifting relations between them as high fashion does or does not trickle down through low-cost production of copied designs, for example. But the consumption of clothing does not fit into a general, horizontal theory of consumption, and certainly not one in which all consumption is simultaneously determined by rational calculation across all prices and income. Some such considerations will apply as much to the food as to the fashion system. But, in itself, and across individual foods, how food systems function and how they reproduce (or transform) themselves both materially and culturally differs considerably over time, place and context with, for example, fair trading and ethical concerns differentially coming to the fore in the current period in some respects. In this light, analysis of consumption cannot be divorced from the systems of production to which it is attached, not just because they set prices for goods but because they are driven by the imperative of profitability that leads to changes in the nature of what is provided and corresponding attitudes to this by consumers. As suggested, the integral nature of what and how we consume depends on what and how it is provided, and how and why we consume it. This is complex and diverse across items of consumption. But, precisely because commodity production for profit is, in general, the source for the vast majority of consumption, so how such commodities come to the market in large quantities and how they are accepted as such for the purposes of consumption, form the rationale for examining consumption in terms of distinct material and cultural systems of provision.[7]

2.7 Broader Implications

Consumer theory is paramount to neoclassical orthodoxy for two separate reasons. On the one hand, and most obviously, in a sense it represents half of a discipline that organises itself around supply and demand. Get demand wrong and more or less everything else is going to be wrong however well you deal with the supply side. On the other hand, consumer theory is representa-

---

7. Neoclassical consumer theory can handle different goods as being more or less independent of one another in terms of levels of demand (subject to budget constraint across all goods) and does so in terms of what it calls separability. But this will be something that is assumed in the underlying preferences, not something that is explained.

tive of the mainstream across a wider terrain than for demand alone, not least because it takes the optimising individual as its starting point. In this respect, the weaknesses and fragilities of consumer theory are indicative of the frailties across the discipline as a whole, as can be seen in a number of ways.

First is to recognise that there is a strict correspondence between consumer and producer theory as can be shown in two different ways, especially when stripped down to technical content. The consumer, for example, can be interpreted as a producer running their own firm in minimising the cost of producing a given level of utils at prevailing inputs prices for consumer goods (as is evident from the Hicksian demand functions). Strikingly, the indifference curves through which this is represented are identical to the isoquants for which producers minimise the cost of producing a given level of output. As indicated, Diagram 2.1 could be isoquants with output levels, not indifference curves with utility levels. In this respect, consumer and producer theory are the same, and the core principles of marginalism are reduced to a single diagram. Second, there is a major difference between consumer theory and producer theory in that the latter has become much richer on the basis of the same initiating technical apparatus. The reason for this is of interest, for producer theory has used that apparatus to seek to address a whole series of problems associated with the functioning of the capitalist economy, ranging in particular over the different ways in which firms compete with one another (see Chapter 4). The point here is not how well this is done, and it remains marked by its starting point (production functions, given technology, etc.) much as consumer theory does (with given preferences and goods). Rather, the sorts of economic processes attached to supply, such as the entry and exit of firms to forge long-run equilibrium, cannot be embraced in relation to consumer theory since consumers are not like firms in this respect, subject to (competitive) entry and exit however well understood (although there are theories of fertility and mortality that treat them as if consumer choice).

Third, this points to the failure of the orthodoxy to address the creation of consumers, whether by themselves or through social processes, in anything other than a token fashion. This is why consumer theory has stagnated conceptually within economics over a hundred years or more, as discussed in the opening remarks to this chapter, whereas it has blossomed across the other social sciences. For this to be otherwise, economics as a whole would have to be radically transformed across its neglect of, and contempt for, the history of economic thought, its limited knowledge and account of its own let alone other methodologies, its intolerance of heterodoxy, and its failure to address interdisciplinarity adequately.

Fourth, this all reveals the extreme intellectual fragility characteristic of mainstream economics. The introduction or reintroduction of the factors, which were excluded in order that it might be established in the first place, reveal how limited it is, most obviously in relation to methodology, history of economic thought, interdisciplinarity and heterodox alternatives. In case of consumption, this is blatant in terms of the core assumptions concerning the given and limited nature of goods and individuals, quite apart from the absence of social determinants. Yet, as indicated through discussion of the latest phase of economics imperialism, the technical apparatus associated with consumer theory (and producer theory as well) is being extended over a wider range of subject matter, both economic and non-economic.

Fifth, this is not only a paradox or irony, insofar as has been observed, that an apparatus that was established for narrow purposes by excluding so many factors, should then be used to explain what has been set aside – it also opens up considerable tensions around the borders of economics and possibly within those borders. For, the more economics applies its reductionist techniques across a wider scope, the more it exposes its limitations. Some have argued that this is liable to lead to the dissolution of the orthodoxy and its replacement by what is currently on its fringes, heterodoxies dealing in behavioural economics, game theory, and the like, especially as considerations from other social sciences are incorporated into economics.

Sixth, there are, however, strong arguments against this view. Mainstream economics has always displayed considerable resilience in the face of the wide-ranging inconsistencies and tensions that it incorporates. It has done so by relying heavily on its technical apparatus of utility and production functions, and retaining these as a priority over resolving inconsistencies whether of a theoretical, conceptual, technical or empirical nature. This is obvious in light of the nature of its treatment of consumption and the extension of that treatment to what is not consumption let alone not even the economic. As much as possible is made reducible to utility-maximising, even at the expense of inconsistency, incoherence, methodological inadequacy and massive empirical anomalies.

There are two ways in which the orthodoxy has traditionally excused, and even prided, itself for these devastating inadequacies. First is to make claims to mathematical rigour as a result of its axiomatic deductivism of which consumer theory is a leading illustration. But, as has been seen, the application of the theory of the optimising consumer is highly inconvenient. It positively shows that all sorts of unacceptable assumptions need to be made for preferences to be represented by a utility function, and for that utility function to be optimised in a well-behaved way. Further, setting this aside still leaves the problem of how aggregating over optimising individuals leads to well-defined aggregate demand curves on prices and income, unless essentially the assumption is made that society is constituted of a single individual with a single indifference curve. And, once interrogated on these terms, the axiomatics do reveal the extent to which the understandings of consumption, the consumer and the consumed are reduced.

Second, the use of econometrics plays a major role in economics, less in testing theories, and estimating parameters, as the conventional wisdom would have it, and more in blundering over methodological, conceptual and theoretical inadequacies. The way in which the econometrics is done is often as clumsy and arbitrary as the theory. And the idea that this in some sense mirrors the methods of the natural sciences, a rigour in empirical methods to parallel its mathematical methods, is laughable. The natural sciences do not base their assumptions on speculative reasoning governed by an unchallenged technical apparatus and then deduce outcomes for empirical testing. Rather, the assumptions themselves are often closely empirically investigated and interact with the process of theory construction and investigation. This is not to say that economics should seek to emulate the methods of the natural sciences but, for consumption in particular, and the economy more generally, starting points should be made in capital, capitalism, power, conflict, class, etc., with these attached to historical specificity and the cultures of consumption and the consumed in the practices of the situated consumer. In other words, for an economics of consumption to prosper, it must involve political economy and, or as, interdisciplinarity.

2.8 Further Thoughts and Readings

I have investigated the theories and the determinants of consumption extensively, most notably in Fine (2002), see also Fine and Leopold (1993), with coverage across a number of disciplines, topics and case studies. This volume also presents the system of provision approach in detail, for which see also Fine (2013b) and Bayliss et al. (2013). For a critique of the mainstream approach to identity, see Fine (2009) and also Davis (2011).

3

From Production to Supply and Beyond to General Equilibrium?

3.1 Overview

This chapter begins in Section 3.2 by outlining the mainstream theory of supply. It finds that there are strict parallels in a formal, technical sense, with the theory of demand. Although the individual firm has the motive of maximising profits, it too must minimise the cost of producing what output it produces, just as the consumer minimises the cost of attaining utility. As a result, the production for the firm is very similar to the utility function for the consumer, although there is the added difference of maximising profits, deciding how much to produce as well as how to produce it from available inputs. Not surprisingly, then, there is a correspondence between the Marshallian and Hicksian systems of demand and of supply, although there are some differences. Nonetheless, despite different ways of approaching supply, through cost functions and profit functions for example, these are all shown to be equivalent to one another and reducible to the specification of a production function, which is itself reduced to a simple relationship between inputs and outputs.

In Section 3.3, supply and demand are put together across all individuals and markets simultaneously to address the problem of general equilibrium. This is shown to falter over problems of existence, uniqueness, Pareto efficiency and stability unless extraordinarily restrictive assumptions are made even on the terms of the mainstream itself. Much the same is true of the two fundamental theorems of welfare economics, whether any Pareto efficient outcome can be a general equilibrium and whether any general equilibrium is Pareto efficient. Again, because of the stringent conditions necessary for such results, their relevance for understanding the economy for this and other reasons (including the so-called theory of the second best) seems to hang on less than a single thread. Nonetheless, having gone to so much trouble to obtain general equilibrium as the pinnacle of achievement of the technical apparatus and technical architecture of microeconomics (TA^2), economics has continued to proceed as if its threadbare existence is of no consequence as an organising principle.

3.2 Production and Cost Functions Rule, OK?

Many students will first meet the theory of supply in the form of a cost function, $C(q)$, where C is the cost of supplying quantity q. With a given price for output p, the profit-maximising firm will set marginal cost equal to price, $C'(q) = p$, with profit maximum (as opposed to minimum) as long as $C''(q)$ is negative at the profit-maximising output. This leaves many questions unanswered. On the cost side, why are costs the way they are, how does production take place, and with what inputs and technology? On the price side, why is the price at the level that it is, and why should it be taken as given?

The assumption of given prices is usually justified by appeal to perfect competition (see Chapter 4). It is presumed that if a firm increases its price, it will lose all sales to competitors, and reducing price will reduce potential profits. On this basis, fixed prices as a result of competition are taken as a standard starting point for the theory of supply. On the cost side, the theory of production takes a production function, $q = f(x_1, x_2, x_3, ..., x_n)$ as its starting point, where $x_1, x_2, x_3, ..., x_n$ are the inputs needed to produce output q. Many students will also be familiar with this formulation, especially with the idea that the marginal product of a factor input, x_i will be set equal to its relative price for the cost-minimising firm, $f_i = p_i/p$, where p is the given price of the output, as long as marginal products are decreasing, $f_{ii} < 0$. This requires that input prices, p_i, as well as output price, p, are competitive insofar as firms can buy as many inputs as they like at the given prices, p_i, and sell at price p as much as they like of the output they make with those inputs.

To some degree, the assumptions that have been made already could be relaxed. Smoothly differentiable production and cost functions are not strictly necessary. Also, allowance could be made for joint production, more than one type of output from the inputs rather than a single output, q. This will all be set aside in order to simplify the presentation of technical details in what follows. But, before engaging in the technicalities, it is worth reminding ourselves of the extent to which the theory of supply is reduced, for a number of reasons related to the requirements of deriving a theory of supply from the technical apparatus attached to the production function.

First, as is apparent from the formalities, the theory of production is universal and, correspondingly, asocial and ahistorical. It could prevail in any circumstances across any sector and context. Indeed, production is reduced to a simple relationship between inputs and outputs without regard to what these inputs and outputs are, and without an examination of the production process itself – who does what and how. There is even a total absence of human agency in two respects (apart from the presumed profit-maximising entrepreneur). On the one hand, there are no bosses with no one telling others what to do (although entrepreneurship might be considered to be one of the inputs, x_i). On the other hand, labour and workers occupy no special place in the theory, being designated as an input like any other. So they are bought at a price, presumably the wage, and used as an input just like any other (with marginal product of labour set equal to the real wage). In a similar way to the theory of consumption and demand, inputs as well as outputs have no specificity precisely in order to enable them to be expressed formally in undifferentiated mathematical form. There must even be doubts about whether this represents production in any meaningful sense, as it is reduced to 'something goes in' and 'something comes out' and could correspond to any quantitative process of this type, a chemical reaction for example – put in hydrogen and oxygen and you get water!

Second, by the same token, not only is technology taken as given (by the production function f), it too is not specified, potentially ranging from simple peasant farming to high-tech methods. There is no account of where technology comes from and how it might change.

Third, related to but distinct from the previous points, there is no consideration of how production is organised (and the same applies to distribution and sale). Whilst there is a presumption of wage labour (and production for profit), this is not even implicit within the production function itself. Does it not make a difference if production is organised as wage labour for the production of commodities that are going to be sold, as opposed to domestic production for own use for example, or even a squirrel running around gathering nuts with its labouring time and tree inputs? Fourth, the assumption of perfect competition is made in order that individual optimisation can take place without needing to second-guess what other individuals might or might not be doing. Prices of outputs and inputs can be taken as given.

Fifth, even with these assumptions already in place, it is still necessary to impose restrictions on production conditions in order that the optimisation can be satisfactorily achieved. There must be decreasing returns to factors or to scale overall, otherwise, for given input and output prices, it is more profitable to increase output indefinitely, as profits just go on increasing the more you produce and sell.

Bearing these considerations in mind, the theory of production is heavily determined by the production function, f. It can be used in a number of familiar ways. First is to minimise costs of producing a given output, q. Formally:

Minimise $C = p_1 x_1 + ... + p_n x_n$ subject to $f(x_1, ..., x_n) = q$.

If this problem is solved (through use of the Lagrange multiplier for example, see Box 3.1), Hicksian conditional (on given output q) input demands will be derived. These correspond to the Hicksian conditional, or compensated, consumer demand in which a fixed utility is required at minimum expenditure (see Chapter 2). Accordingly, h_i tells us the demand for input x_i in minimising cost to produce output q with input prices, p_i:

$$x_i = h_i(q, p_1, ..., p_n).$$

Input demands will in general depend on their relative prices and how much is produced (at minimum cost). These input demand functions have certain properties. They will be increasing in q (more demand for inputs to produce more output); they will be homogeneous of degree 1 in the prices (double all input prices and you double your costs but purchase the same inputs); and they will be decreasing in own price.

Having derived input demands, the minimum cost can now be found by adding up inputs costs to give the cost function, $C = C(q, p_1, ..., p_n)$. In its simplest form, this is the familiar cost function, $C = C(q)$, where input prices are taken as permanently fixed and drop away from the function. More generally, in allowing input prices to vary explicitly, it follows that C is increasing in q (it costs more to produce more); homogeneous of degree 1 in input prices (if you double all prices, costs will double); and convex in prices (increasing in input prices but less than or equal in proportion because, if input prices change, the worse you could do in producing a given output is to use those inputs you are already using, and so cost can only go up in proportion to the prices themselves and you might do better by changing your input mix).

Further, the minimum cost to produce output is entirely analogous to the minimum cost to produce a given level of utility, merely substituting f for u. It follows that the cost function, C, for a given output, q, is analogous to the expenditure function, I, from Chapter 2 (for a given utility), u. And Shephard's lemma also applies so that we can more or less paraphrase from our demand theory for our producer or supply theory. From Shephard's lemma, $h_i = \delta C/\delta p_i$, i.e. the extra cost to produce from an increase in an input price, is primarily the result of the extra cost of the inputs you are already using (with substitution into less expensive inputs of lesser-order significance). Further, because of the pure substitution effect, in moving around an isoquant in response to changing relative input prices, $\delta h_i/\delta p_j$ should be positive unless i = j in which case it is negative.

In addition, because the order of differentiation does not make any difference to outcome, $\delta^2 C/\delta p_i \delta p_j = \delta h_j/\delta p_i = \delta h_i/\delta p_j = \delta^2 C/\delta p_j \delta p_i$, and these are all positive unless i = j for which they are negative (otherwise, not a minimum from first-order conditions). In other words, substituting along, or around, an isoquant from one input, i, to another input, j, is equal and opposite to going the other way around, and is positive (as with indifference curves as opposed to isoquants).

Box 3.1
Lagrange optimisation

Lagrange optimisation is concerned with maximising or minimising when there is a constraint on the values that can be taken by variables. A typical example is to minimise the cost of producing a given level of output q, with production function $f(x_1, x_2, ..., x_n)$ where x_i are inputs with prices, p_i. Formally:

Minimise $C = p_1 x_1 + p_2 x_2 + ... + p_n x_n$ subject to $q - f(x_1, x_2, ..., x_n) = 0$.

The way this problem is solved is to form the Langrangean,

$L = p_1 x_1 + p_2 x_2 + ... + p_n x_n + \lambda(q - f(x_1, x_2, ..., x_n))$

where λ is called the Lagrange multiplier. The Langrangean is now minimised over the $n + 1$ variables, made up of x_i and λ. This gives:

$dL/dx_i = p_i - \lambda f_i = 0$

so that $f_i = p_i/\lambda$, and note that $f_i/f_j = p_i/p_j$ or relative marginal products equal relative input prices, and

$dL/d\lambda = q - f = 0$,

which is the original constraint.

There are also second-order conditions to satisfy but these will not be covered here (although they are important for Slutsky–Hicks–Samuelson conditions). Why does Lagrange work? The minimum derived must be at least lower than for the constrained optimisation because λ could always be chosen to be zero and the x_i are free to be chosen. But, in optimising for L, the constraint is satisfied and the optimal value of L equals C because of this. So optimal L cannot be lower other than for the constrained optimisation. So, as it is neither higher nor lower than the constrained problem, the freely optimised L gives the solution.

But what is λ? Suppose that instead of the constraint q as the output to be produced, it is increased by a small amount, dq. To produce this, it is necessary to increase inputs so that:

$dq = f_1 dx_1 + f_2 dx_2 + ... + f_n dx_n = p_1 dx_1/\lambda + p_2 dx_2/\lambda + ... + p_n dx_n/\lambda = dC/\lambda$

Thus, $\lambda = dC/dq$. This means that λ equals the extra marginal cost of producing more output. So λ is the change in what you are optimising if you change the constraint – in this case the cost of producing more output. This is true more generally. Whatever is being optimised subject to constraint, the Lagrange multiplier will be the value of changing the constraint at the margin in terms of the outcome of your optimum. For this reason, λ is called the shadow price of relaxing the constraint. It is a price in the sense of a valuation of changing the constraint, and it is a shadow because it does not appear on the market as such (or if it does it is a market price as such rather than the value to you of the item). Thus, for example, if the problem was to maximise utility, u, subject to a budget constraint, $p_1 x_1 + p_2 x_2 + ... + p_n x_n = I$, then λ would be equal to du/dI or the marginal utility of income.

Now it turns out that (alongside homogeneity, etc., already discussed) these properties of the Hicksian demand functions are just necessary and sufficient for them to have been derived from the optimising behaviour of the cost-minimising firm. This means that we can work with the Hicksian demand for inputs for theoretical problems, and use the mathematical properties of the system for the purposes of comparative statics (the properties of a new equilibrium in case of a change in the tariffs on inputs for example). We can also take a proposed Marshallian demand system (see below), transform it into its Hicksian counterpart and check that it satisfies the necessary and sufficient conditions for being derived from optimising behaviour. In that way, when empirically estimating the Marshallian system from observed data, it can be confirmed that a properly constituted demand curve is in play. Alternatively, a Hicksian demand system can be taken and translated into a Marshallian system for estimation.

But the Marshallian system has not yet been laid out, for which the goal is not to minimise production costs for a given output as such but to maximise profits directly. Returning to the production function, instead of minimising costs of producing a given output, consider maximising profits directly. Formally:

Maximise $\Pi = pq - (p_1 x_1 + ... + p_n x_n)$ where $q = f(x_1, ..., x_n)$, or
Maximise $\Pi = pf(x_1, ..., x_n) - (p_1 x_1 + ... + p_n x_n)$.

This can be done directly through solving the first-order conditions for which:

$pf_i(x_i) = p_i$ or $f_i(x_i) = p_i/p$.

This is the familiar notion that the marginal product of x_i should equal its relative price for profit maximisation. From n such equations, one each for each input, i, the unconditional Marshallian input demands can be derived. These go straight for profit maximising (rather than minimum cost for a given level of output) and so are functions of output and input prices. The demand for input x_i is given by:

$x_i = x_i(p, p_1, ..., p_n)$.

These can be plugged into the production function to derive the level of output, or the supply function S, contingent upon input and output prices:

$$S = S(p, p_1, ..., p_n).$$

And, ultimately, a profit function Π can be derived:

$$\Pi = \Pi(p, p_1, ..., p_n) \text{ since } \Pi = pS - \Sigma p_i x_i.$$

Again, Π will have various properties. From Hotelling's lemma, it follows that both $\delta\Pi/\delta p = S$, the supply function, and $\delta\Pi/\delta p_i = -x_i$, the Marshallian input demands.

This is as far as can be gone with the production function as the starting point. It has allowed a cost function and a profit function to be derived. Yet, it would be equally possible to start with a cost function, $C(q, p_1, ..., p_n)$ and set about maximising profits $\Pi = pq - C(q, p_1, ..., p_n)$, by choosing q for given p and p_i, to derive the profit function. All of this is summarised in Diagram 3.1. It parallels the one for consumer theory, Diagram 2.3, with the various different approaches within producer theory seen to be more or less equivalent to one another. As a result, it follows that the theory of production, or supply, is totally dependent upon the production function, f, as for u for consumer theory (see Diagram 2.3). The technical apparatus is deployed to derive the necessary results. It is also possible to see that all the different approaches to supply around cost, supply, profit and production functions, let alone isoquants, are more or less equivalent to one another.

In short, the production function, f, occupies a central position in the microeconomics of supply just as does the utility function, u, in consumer theory. As for the latter, it originates and derives from a particular problem, the theory of supply (and demand for inputs) within the context of the market and the profit-maximising entrepreneur. Having been established and fully explored for this purpose in conditions of perfect competition (to obtain cost and profit functions as well as input demand functions), the production function is found to be universal in its substantive content and, correspondingly, scope of application. After all, $q = f(x_1, ..., x_n)$ has nothing as such to do with q as either output or with x_i as input on the market: f can stand for anything, as can q and x_i.

Such is the historical logic once more of economics imperialism. And, equally, from the implosion in deriving core microeconomic results, in the passage from the marginalist to the formalist revolutions, subsequently there is an explosion of use of such microeconomic principles across the discipline and, if lesser and later, other social sciences. Thus, for example, human capital theory (and its application) is very much tied to the idea of production functions. This not only involves reducing skills to an input into a production process like anything else but, equally, this is the way that skills are understood as being produced with

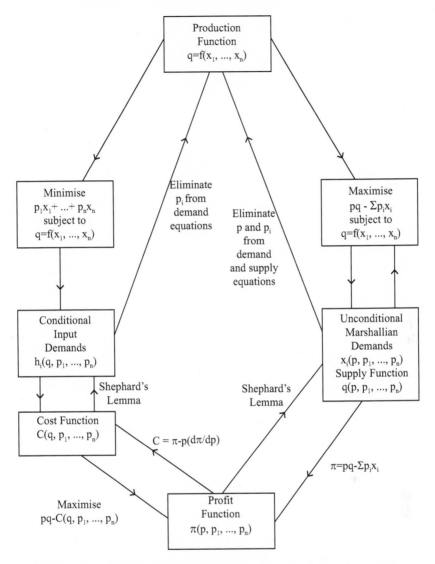

Diagram 3.1 The complete and closed system of neoclassical producer theory

(ultimately for example) schools or other training being perceived as subject to a production function (see Chapter 6).

Not surprisingly, given the universal applicability of the production function, its use is readily extended to any unit of production, from the original firm to sectors, regions and national economies. Most notably in growth theory, and in other applications too including a huge swathe of macroeconomics, a single production function comes to be used to represent aggregate supply with a whole host of associated theoretical and empirical problems (see Chapter 5).

Equally, at the level of the firm, once the production function is established it becomes the basis for exploring what was necessarily taken out in order to establish it in the first place. Accordingly, the attempt is made to open up what is known as the black box of the firm. Why do firms even exist? Why are there hierarchies within them? Once again, as with economics imperialism more generally, these processes of BBI what has been excluded are increasingly based on the idea of market imperfections, especially asymmetric information. In this way, industrial relations becomes reduced to problems of incomplete information, or enforcement of (labour) contracts (balancing the costs of workers slacking against the costs of monitoring or disciplining them more closely). In other words, how do we realise the potential of a production function given the intrusion of labour relations when production itself has already been conceived of as taking place in the absence of such relations?

Similar considerations arise in the case of technology, taken as absent in constructing the production function. Then, of course, having got the production function in the absence of a given technology, technological change can then be brought back in on the basis of production functions. Most obviously, new technology can be conceived as being produced with a production function for it, dependent on inputs of resources dedicated to innovation for example. Or technological change can be taken as a market imperfection, arising for example out of externalities (which were excluded to construct TA^2), with learning-by-doing on the job or productivity spin-offs between firms. These approaches raise the conundrum that, if such factors are known in advance, why are they not incorporated into the optimising processes? And, if not known in advance, the conditions do not hold for TA^2 to be appropriate. This all points again to the inconsistency, incoherence even, of both excluding factors to establish your principles and then using those principles to examine what has been excluded. The problems arise from privileging a set of principles in deriving some results in a very narrowly defined, even flawed, context and then seeking to extend those principles far beyond their initial confines.

3.3 General Equilibrium: A Fantasy Glass, Half Empty or Half Full?

As has been demonstrated, most clearly in the parallel between indifference curves and isoquants, the theory of (consumer) demand and of (producer) supply are very close to one another, especially in formal terms. It is as if the economics of the individual can be reduced to Diagram 2.1 only. Microeconomics, however, completed its TA^2 by putting many individuals together for their demand and supply and adding up the supplies and demands of those individuals to determine a perfectly competitive price level at which supply and demand are equal to one another in aggregate simultaneously in each market.

It is helpful to trace this out, first for a single producer and consumer – the so-called Robinson Crusoe model, in which Robinson behaves as both producer and consumer with a split personality without realising, since liaising with himself through the market. As a consumer, suppose Robinson has utility function, $u(x, l)$, where x is the consumption of the single consumer good and l is the amount of leisure. It will be assumed that Robinson must divide his time between being at work, fishing or whatever, which provides him with goods to sell (to himself as it happens), or that he is at leisure, providing him with utility. Diagram 3.2 shows his indifference curves. These are slightly unusual since the graphs are to some extent backwards. This is because work on the x-axis counts negatively towards utility as the opposite of leisure.

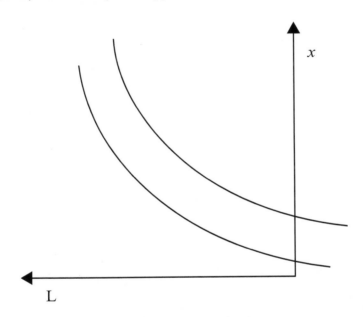

Diagram 3.2   Robinson's utility

Now the production function for Robinson will be $f(L)$ where L is the amount of leisure he sacrifices, leaving him $24 - L$ hours left in the day for leisure, l, depending on how you treat sleep and other (in)activities necessary for life let alone work and leisure themselves. It is assumed that f is increasing with diminishing marginal product, as illustrated in Diagram 3.3.

It follows that Robinson must choose to be somewhere on his production function. The question is where? The obvious answer is the point at which he gets on to his highest indifference curve. This is represented as G in Diagram 3.4. G is Pareto efficient (see Box 3.2), as going anywhere else that is feasible would make Robinson worse off, necessarily not making anyone else better off since there is no one else. This is because Robinson can at most go somewhere

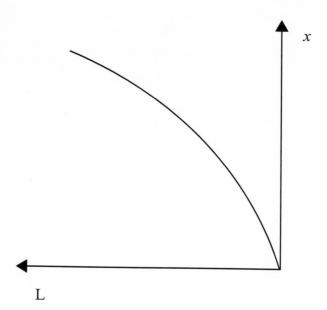

Diagram 3.3   Robinson's production

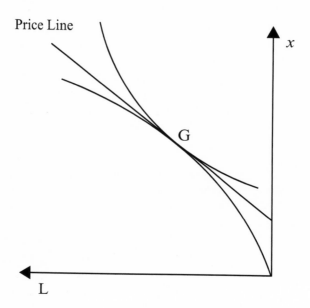

Diagram 3.4   Robinson's optimum

Box 3.2
Pareto efficiency

A state of the world is said to be Pareto efficient (or alternatively Pareto optimal) if, compared to all other possible outcomes, no one can be made better off without someone else being made worse off. Pareto efficiency is often seen by economists as a more or less uncontroversial criterion for choosing between options. Surely, it is better to have someone better off if no one else is made worse off (as would be the case if an outcome were Pareto inefficient).

But the appeal to economists of Pareto efficiency betrays some strong assumptions and tensions. Many economists see what they do as positive economics, as opposed to normative economics, by which they mean free of value judgements. But commitment to Pareto efficiency is far from value neutral. First, it is strongly based on a particular version of what is taken to underpin utilitarianism, that the value of a society is based primarily, or purely, on the value of that society to its members taken as individuals. Second, individuals themselves are taken to be the best judges of whether they are better off or not. This would hardly be considered acceptable if individuals were brainwashed, temporarily insane or under the influence of drugs, etc. Things need not be so extreme, but this points to the need to know why and how individuals are better off if a judgement is to be made on whether this makes for a better state of the world, let alone their own welfare of which they might not be in the best position to assess – without, thereby, descending into being either patronising or authoritarian.

This, then, is not to go to the opposite extreme of insisting that assessment of individual welfare should be undertaken independently of the individuals concerned or imposed by reference to externally determined criteria. Rather it is simply to acknowledge that outcomes must in part be judged on the basis of how they are brought about, including individuals' assessments of their own well-being as better off or not (a view they might change if encouraged to speculate on why they consider themselves to be better off or not in different circumstances). A third, related but distinct, point is that our assessment of different alternative outcomes can be based on the nature of society and not just individual welfare within that society. There are criteria of equality, fairness and justice to consider quite apart, even at the individual level, from concern for others.

Some of these points can be illustrated by a simple example of inequality. Let us suppose that there is a huge number of people whose welfare is represented numerically. Let everyone have the same welfare and compare this with a situation in which everyone has the same except for one who has more. Are we prepared to sacrifice a commitment to equality irrespective of whether the individual's extra is small or large? If the extra is small, so is the gain for the individual relative to the sacrifice of equality for the society. And if the extra is very large, the individual concerned is both going to breach the principle of equality and have a very privileged position in relation to others. And, once more, do we want to commit to Pareto efficiency irrespective of how the levels of welfare have been obtained and what motivates them?

beneath the production function and, given this, his highest attainable point in terms of indifference curves is G.

We could simply instruct Robinson to go to G or allow him to discover G for himself. But is there a market mechanism by which Robinson would choose to settle at G? The answer is yes, as demonstrated in Diagram 3.4. The (relative) price line for goods and wages prices represented by the tangent to both indifference curve and production function at G will do the trick. If such prices are set, and Robinson receives the profit of his work as owner of the firm but spends it as a consumer, then he will go to G independently both as a maximising-utility consumer and as a profit-maximising producer, and supply and demand of both goods and labour will be equal.

Such is possibly the simplest demonstration of a general equilibrium: a set of prices at which supply equals demand in each market. There are two important properties involved. One is simply the existence of the general equilibrium. This has been possible in this case because of the ability to force the price line between the indifference curve and the production function, touching each tangentially without its intersecting with either anywhere else (otherwise the optimising Robinson, as either producer or consumer, would go elsewhere other than G, since profits or utility, respectively, would be higher there whilst staying on the budget line). It can be seen immediately that, if the indifference curves and production were differently shaped, this separating price line would not necessarily exist. It would be impossible, for example, if the production function exhibited increasing returns to scale, or was concave rather than convex to the

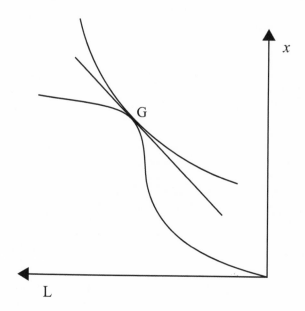

Diagram 3.5   General equilibrium with (some) increasing returns

origin. In other words, it is not necessary to have smoothly shaped curves but they do have to be amenable to getting a price line between them where they touch for there to be a general equilibrium at the point of touching. However, see Diagram 3.5 for some increasing returns but not enough to prevent a general equilibrium.

This analysis gives rise to what has been called the two fundamental theorems of welfare economics (itself an indication of the extent to which 'welfare' has been reduced in its meaning). For the first of these, the theorem suggests that, under certain conditions, a competitive general equilibrium will be Pareto efficient. The conditions required are relatively weak, compared to the second theorem. It is not necessary, for example, to exclude increasing returns to scale. The reason is that the theorem can become vacuous in this case, as a general equilibrium will not exist and the theorem becomes true by default. Each general equilibrium is Pareto efficient because there is none. There could also be some increasing returns at low levels of production and still allow for a Pareto efficient general equilibrium, as in Diagram 3.5. Hardly surprisingly, though, what is needed for the theorem, over and above the underlying axioms of fixed utility and production functions, given prices and optimising individuals, is that there should be no externalities. If there are externalities, a general equilibrium is not going to be Pareto efficient, as taking the externalities into account could improve outcomes rather than relying upon individual optimisation that ignores them, with more or less activity by individuals being desirable depending upon whether externalities are positive or negative, respectively. Robinson as a producer might pollute his environment as a consumer for example. And he might, as a consumer, even enjoy the activity of labour, such as fishing, which he deplores as a worker as a loss of leisure.

The second fundamental theorem of welfare economics is the converse of the first. It suggests that a Pareto efficient outcome is capable of being supported by a general equilibrium (as long as assets are distributed appropriately to individuals). This, however, does require that there should be no increasing returns (as well as no externalities). The reason is apparent from Diagram 3.6. Here P does represent a Pareto efficient outcome for Robinson but no price mechanism will support this outcome as it is impossible to get a price line to separate the indifference curve and production function where they touch (essentially because the curvature on the indifference curve is greater than the increasing returns, allowing for Pareto efficiency but not for general equilibrium – for a mutually tangential price line at P, utility will be maximised but profits minimised).

Interpretation of the two fundamental theorems of welfare economics, on their own terms, is open to a glass half full versus glass half empty syndrome. For the first theorem, the positive interpretation is that, putatively following Adam Smith's invisible hand, it is ok to leave everything to the market as the

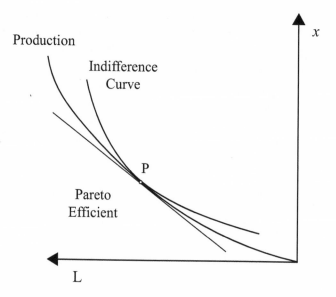

Diagram 3.6　　Pareto efficiency without general equilibrium

outcome will be Pareto efficient. This, though, heavily overlooks the fact that general equilibrium has no role in Adam Smith's political economy whatsoever (it is simply a reinvention in retrospect of the history of economic thought through a neoclassical prism). As shown in Chapter 4, Adam Smith is much more concerned with the role of the expansion of the market in providing for economies of scale and productivity increase through an increasing division of labour as the source of the 'wealth of nations'.

Although, as observed, the first theorem still holds in case there are increasing returns, this is of little consolation since there will be no general equilibrium for the market to attain (even though Adam Smith did consider falsely, by extrapolating from a single sector to the economy as a whole, that capitalism would end up in a 'stationary state' with minimal profit, once productivity increase exhausted market demand). In a sense, this is even the basis for taking the pessimistic view of the first theorem. For the necessary conditions under which the theorem holds are particularly stringent, not least requiring the total absence of any externalities and of any other distortions from perfect competition. From this perspective, the first theorem offers an interesting exception or even a standard against which the real world is to be judged.

In short, the chances that the real world does or can correspond to general equilibrium are miniscule. That it might be used as a standard against which to judge the world, though, is somewhat bizarre. It is as if the mythical figure of the unicorn is constructed in order to understand the nature of the horse, one without a horn!

The second theorem is also open to positive and negative interpretations along the same sort of lines. Suppose a desirable, Pareto efficient outcome is identified. Is it possible for the market mechanism to place the economy at that outcome? Subject to an appropriate (re)distribution of resources to individuals, the answer is yes – as long as there is an absence of externalities, increasing returns, etc. Such a positive take on the potential of the market to deliver desirable outcomes was even deployed in the 1930s and beyond by socialists against embryonic neoliberals in the 'market socialism' debate (although it is a moot point whether the terms of the debate had much to say about the realities or potential nature of socialism itself). On the other hand, of course, the conditions necessary for a Pareto efficient outcome to be delivered by general equilibrium are particularly stringent.

Such considerations become even more demanding in complexity and substance once moving beyond the simple representation of general equilibrium drawing upon a single individual, Robinson, and a single input, labour or more exactly loss of leisure, and single output – although the addition of the enslaved Man Friday hardly satisfies the background conditions of optimising individuals engaging freely in the market. In principle, of course, it is conceptually undemanding to go to a world of many individuals and many goods. For the individuals, we can aggregate over their individual supply and demand curves and, for many goods, the outcomes can be tackled in terms of the earlier presentations around supply and demand (and production and utility functions).

To find a general equilibrium in these circumstances, it is necessary to generalise across finding a price line that tangentially separates an individual indifference curve from an individual isoquant (as in the simpler case illustrated earlier in relation to Diagram 3.4). In many dimensions, this involves finding what is called a separating hyperplane, in which each and every individual's indifference curves and isoquants are separated as well as aggregate supplies equating to aggregate demand (you might be able to imagine this in an extension to three dimensions rather than two). In 1954, Arrow and Debreu eventually proved the existence of general equilibrium under conditions similar to those made for the simpler case covered earlier (see Diagram 3.4). The proof essentially involved putting the following intuition into rigorous mathematical argument. For any good, its excess demand is liable to be positive when its price is low, and to be negative as long as the price is made high enough. So by moving prices up (down) if there is excess demand (supply), a set of prices will eventually emerge in which all supplies will equal demand. Indeed, this is the sort of argument (dubbed *tâtonnement* or 'groping') used by Léon Walras to justify general equilibrium in the 1870s (although the Marshallian partial dominated over general equilibrium in microeconomics until the late 1930s when Walras was rediscovered).

Could general equilibrium theory breathe a huge sigh of relief once its existence had been established? The answer is not really, quite apart from the issues raised by the conditions necessary for its existence and Pareto efficiency. This is because of two other conditions for its practical relevance even on its own terms, those of uniqueness and stability. In case of lack of uniqueness, how would we know whether we were at one general equilibrium as opposed to another. And, even if unique, an unstable general equilibrium would be of limited practical relevance. So could uniqueness and stability be shown to hold for general equilibrium?

The answer is essentially in the negative unless even more stringent conditions hold. Go back to the *tâtonnement*. This would appear to direct us towards a unique equilibrium (because of high demand at low prices and low demand at high prices and so bringing supply and demand together by shifting prices up or down, respectively). But this is only because it has implicitly been presumed that there are no inferior goods. As is known only too well, if negative income effects outweigh substitution effects, demand may well increase with price. Whilst high demand at the lowest prices, and low demand at the highest prices, are sufficient to guarantee at least one equilibrium between these extremes, a unique equilibrium cannot be guaranteed, as excess demand functions may wobble up and down as prices change. In short, the only way to guarantee a unique equilibrium is to insist that all goods are what are termed gross substitutes for one another, essentially that there are no weighty inferior goods within the economy.

Very similar considerations apply to the issue of stability. First, though, it is necessary to make a very clear distinction between dynamics and comparative statics. The latter involves a comparison between two equilibria. Suppose, for example, there is a change in the conditions of supply – an increase in a factor endowment (e.g. land) or an improvement in technology, exogenously given. Then the new equilibrium can be contrasted with the old, and this applies to all analyses involving equilibria (whether partial or general within economics or any other application outside of economics, such as mechanics). Terminologically, in comparing equilibria, it is often expressed as a movement from one to the other. Supply increases from x to y, for example. But this is misleading as no movement as such is involved. There is simply comparison of one static equilibrium with another, and there can be no presumption that the exogenous shift in supply, or whatever, leads to a movement from the old to (or even towards) the new equilibrium.

This is the subject matter of dynamics and, of course, such movement between equilibria will depend upon whether the new equilibrium is stable or not. But, in order to assess stability, further assumptions are necessary to be able to investigate how the system responds to being out of equilibrium, bearing in mind that this is not the subject matter of comparative statics which simply investigates when the system (supply and demand for economics) is in balance (not how it moves when it is not). However, the static analysis can itself be highly suggestive of the assumptions to be made for dynamics, not least to rely upon *tâtonnement*. Suppose that price increases in case there is excess demand in a market and decreases if there is excess supply.

The question is whether such dynamics are guaranteed to bring about stability or not – in general, the answer is in the negative. The reason is very similar to the failure of general equilibrium to be unique. The *tâtonnement* is supposed to generate stability by closing excess demand or excess supply by an appropriate movement of prices. But, as has been seen, increasing price where there is excess demand could, in case of inferior goods, bring about an increase in excess demand, undermining the stability of the system. Once again gross substitutes seem to be necessary – to guarantee stability as well as uniqueness.

The same is true for yet another problem, called the 'theory of the second best'. Even if there is a stable, unique, Pareto efficient general equilibrium, the chances are slim that all conditions are satisfied, and a number of them are liable to be violated. Suppose policy or otherwise moves towards, or satisfies the conditions for the equilibrium (for example, moving prices towards marginal utilities in more but not all markets through taxation), then it might be expected that there would be an increase in welfare because of a discrete step, if not complete movement, towards the general equilibrium. This, however, is not the case. If you do not satisfy all of the conditions for general equilibrium, then satisfying more but not all does not necessarily make things better. As a simple metaphor for this, suppose you are on the top of a hill but not of the highest hill. By moving towards the highest hill you could well go down before you go up, and end up lower than before. Such mechanical analogies might be useful in understanding mainstream economics, but whether they are useful in understanding the economy is another matter!

Such results suggest that the half full–half empty metaphor previously deployed is entirely inappropriate, since the jug is almost if not entirely empty as far as the likely satisfaction of the conditions for the fundamental theorems of welfare economics are concerned. But it is as if the weight of effort that has gone into constructing TA² is not to be wasted. Indeed, following the proof of the theorems, there were few other options, so economists set themselves the esoteric, but to some degree technically demanding, exercise of searching out the weakest conditions under which the theorems hold. Despite, in principle, their own demonstration of the extremes of conditions and assumptions that are necessary for TA² to be valid and to underpin the fundamental theorems, it became commonplace to proceed as if they had been legitimised as part of a conventional wisdom for the discipline. And, in line with economics imperialism, the more TA^2 became utilised within economics and across other disciplines, the more powerful it grew as an unquestioned and unquestioning conventional wisdom, with the necessary assumptions and conditions overlooked and/or disregarded.

As has been emphasised, there is a strict parallel between the theories of supply and demand, formally in each being attached to TA^2 and the identity between isoquants and indifference curves, and more informally in the role of the consumer as equivalent to a producer of utility at minimum cost. In Chapter 2, on consumer theory, it was relatively simple to pose alternatives to the mainstream by addressing the issues that it had discarded in establishing itself, particularly those relating to the creation of consumers (genuine subjectivity and identity as opposed to a fixed utility function) and the creation of the meanings of goods. In doing so, it is necessary to engage political economy and interdisciplinarity (and not just to bring back in what has been left out by TA^2 in establishing itself – consumers choosing to maximise their utility by changing their utility functions for example).

A similar path is open in offering alternatives to the theory of supply or production. Why should technology be fixed, what are the social relations under which production takes place, and what are the meanings of corresponding activities to those who undertake them, the worker as opposed to the capitalist? What are the institutional and other non-market mechanisms which both underpin and influence the workings of markets. In consumer and producer theory, these issues are set aside to get at what are considered to be the basics. When it comes to general equilibrium, the extremes to which this leads is revealed by the need to assume that there is a full set of markets; they must exist in all places at all times for all goods (as there is no activity outside of markets), and any other such interactive non-market activity would undermine how supplies and demand are brought into equality with one another through prices.

Even so, setting this all aside, the situation is slightly more complicated for supply and production, as opposed to demand and consumption, for one simple reason. Essentially, consumers are taken as given by the mainstream both in terms of utility functions and in their existence and numbers (unless dealing with the choice of having children – sometimes treated as an investment, sometimes as consumption). The same simply is not true of the theory of supply, since firms, unlike consumers, are allowed not only to compete with one another but also to be born (to enter an industry) and to die (to leave it). This adds a certain richness to the mainstream theory of supply and production that is absent from the theory of consumer demand (consumers competing with one another, if not for pro-creation and survival, might appear to put us in the domain of sociology in competing, or at least keeping up, with the Joneses, or emulation and distinction, and also be in violation of the utility-maximising principle). As a result, the mainstream theory of supply as already presented is complemented by a theory of competition, to be addressed in Chapter 4.

3.4 Further Thoughts and Readings

For a full account of the passage to general equilibrium, see Ingrao and Israel (1990). Some of the other problems with the mainstream theory of production in particular will be raised in subsequent chapters, especially those dealing with competition and technical change.

4
Competition Is
as Competition Does?

4.1 Overview

The conventional view of competition is dominated by what my erstwhile colleague John Weeks has dubbed the quantity theory of competition: the more the number of firms in a sector, the more the degree of competition. This is not only wrong but fundamentally misconceived. As demonstrated by a sequence of models across Sections 4.2–4.9, competition is extremely complex in light of the variety of factors that it incorporates, including price and quantity, collusion, entry and exit (and deterrence), discrimination, and mergers and acquisition, quite apart from the role played by economies of scale and scope, strategising, path dependence, and property rights and transaction costs. Inevitably, the conclusion drawn is not only that there is no relationship between number of firms and competitiveness (and between competitiveness and efficiency) but that even theory, let alone practice, across just one of these factors is incapable of establishing the consequences of more or less competition however this might be interpreted. Accordingly, the implication is not that theory should be eschewed but that it needs to be sensitive to particular circumstances. This result is confirmed in Section 4.10, through a brief excursion into the history of economic thought where, through the contributions of Smith and Marx (on the division of labour), some attention is paid to how competition is contingent on the causes and consequences of productivity increase and, in particular, how the capitalist economy responds in exchange to shifting conditions within production, something that seems to be beyond the mainstream other than through the self-defeating method of comparative statics for which change is reduced to a move from one equilibrium to another.

4.2 Perfect Entry and Exit, and Monopoly

A common starting point for the mainstream theory of competition, as for supply, is a single firm with a given cost function, C, facing 'perfect competition' or a given price for output. From profit maximisation, it follows that marginal cost will be set equal to price, p. So for output, q, $C'(q) = p$, with maximisation only guaranteed by $C''(q) < 0$, or diminishing marginal cost (with profits otherwise expanding with increase in output since costs will be lower and below price). In the context of competition, however, if profits were negative at this maximum it is presumed that the firm would leave the industry. And, if profits were positive, firms can enter.

Here, the notion of competition is being extended from being purely about price-taking to entry into, and exit from, the industry. In this case, profits are supposedly driven down, or up, to zero (taking account of normal profits on capital used up and the 'wages' of entrepreneurship). This raises a new issue for equilibrium: not only how much each firm will produce – given cost function and price – but also how many firms will exist in competitive equilibrium. There is also the issue of how the equilibrium price and quantity will be determined.

The answer to these questions has traditionally been offered in the context of partial equilibrium, only taking account of one sector without interaction with others. The details are familiar from elementary texts. A firm supposedly has a U-shaped marginal cost curve so that marginal cost is actually decreasing to begin with (increasing returns to scale) after which it begins to increase. There is some rationale for this. Set-up costs, for example, are relatively high if you only produce one unit, but these fixed costs can be spread over more units until, eventually, use of the fixed costs is strained and marginal costs begin to increase (see Diagram 4.1).

For the first unit of production, marginal and average costs are the same. Then the average will be larger than marginal costs since the latter are decreasing and

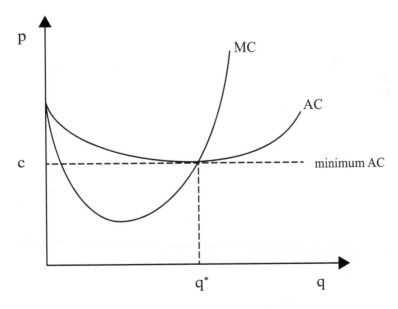

Diagram 4.1   AC = MC at minimum AC

are being shared with 'earlier' higher costs. That is until marginal costs begin to rise and catch up on, and eventually exceed, average costs. This is because the average costs are in part relying upon earlier lower costs rather than purely on the later higher (marginal) costs.

Again, it should be familiar that (the ultimately increasing) marginal and average costs intersect at the point of minimum average cost. The reason for this is that, where the two are equal, if we increase output marginal cost would be greater than average cost and so increase average cost. On the other hand, if we decrease output we would lose a marginal cost lower than average cost, thereby increasing the average cost. As a result, the firm can produce at minimum average cost at the level c, where AC = MC = c, at output q^*. If price, p, is below c, the firm cannot make a profit as average cost exceeds price. Presumably, the firm will exit, reducing industry supply and increasing price. And, if p is above c, the firm can make a positive profit and will produce where MC = p, more than the output at which AC = MC. Presumably such positive profits will induce more firms to enter, thereby increasing supply and reducing prices and profits (to zero or 'normal' levels).

If we interpret perfect competition in terms of freedom of entry and exit, as profits are positive or negative, respectively, it follows that the perfectly competitive price will be $p^* = c$. Otherwise firms will enter, if p > c, and exit, if p < c. Now suppose there is a (partial equilibrium) demand curve for the output given by p = D(Q): then, in perfect competition, there will be an overall level of demand given by $c = D(Q^*)$. Having got Q^*, it will be simple to work out the equilibrium number of firms, n^*, since $n^* = Q^*/q^*$.

For example, suppose the demand curve is p = D – Q, where D is some constant. Then $p^* = c = D - Q^*$; so $Q^* = D - c$, and $n^* = (D - c)/q^*$, where q^* is, as indicated, derived from the cost function, C, where c = AC = MC, or $C'(q^*)$ = $C(q^*)/q^*$. Note that D must be greater than c for this to work. But this is not a problem as D is essentially the most any customer is prepared to pay for just one unit of the output. If this is less than c, the cheapest average cost at which we can produce the good is more than the maximum anyone is prepared to pay for it. Then there is no way the industry can (and should) exist if profits are to be made and the economy is to be efficient.

This is a very satisfying and neat solution. But scratch the surface a little and a number of anomalies arise. First, the equilibrium solution in terms of the number of firms is a slight misnomer. More exactly, it is the number of production units that is being found without any specification of who does or does not own them. It might be that each plant is individually owned and/ or run by somebody unique. But, equally, possibly all of the plants might be owned by the same person which, subject to the extent of free entry, opens up the possibility of some degree of monopoly pricing. So the equilibrium is dependent upon perfect competition to sort out the size of each plant and the ownership structure of the industry, and the two are not exactly the same once moving away from perfect competition.

Second, in the long run there are constant returns to scale for the industry since it is possible to replicate productions costs at c for any scale of production by varying the number of firms. This just guarantees normal profit but, not least in light of the previous point, each firm will be indifferent over how much to produce (or plants to provide) since zero profit will be made at the equilibrium price. If the price were below c, there would be no supply, and supply would be infinite if the price were above c. But at p = c, individual firm output is indeterminate (although there might be expected to be adjustment towards equilibrium should supply not equal demand, thereby driving price away from c).

Third, as observed, the equilibrium (number of firms) depends upon initial increasing returns followed by, ultimately, even stronger decreasing returns. Otherwise, it will be impossible to have an equilibrium. If, for example, there were only diminishing returns, the equilibrium size of the firm would be zero or thereabouts because the cheapest way to produce things would be to have the smallest possible firms and lots of them producing very little. If there were only increasing returns, and average cost does dip below competitive price, then the competitive output would be infinite since the more you produce the more you increase your price–cost margin (as well as the units sold at that margin).

So, the standard shape of marginal and average cost curves is not accidental. They are essential to get at the grinding out of equilibrium both for firm output and number of firms/plants. But this sits uneasily within the theory of general equilibrium for which both increasing and constant returns to scale are a problem. In other words, the partial equilibrium analysis of perfect competition does not fit well with its general equilibrium counterpart. The theory does not seem to allow both for the workings of the economy as a whole and for the dynamics of entry and exit of firms with replicable supply conditions.

Putting this to one side, we will now focus upon partial equilibrium alone as it has more to offer by way of examining competitive behaviour (only entry and exit of firms, or plants, have been considered so far). Consider departing the world of competitive equilibrium. For ease of exposition and as a standard in comparing across different models, suppose that each firm's cost function takes the simple form of $C(q) = F + qc$, where F are fixed costs and c are constant, marginal costs. Here there are increasing returns to scale, since average costs continue to decrease as the fixed costs are shared over ever more output. Whilst $MC = c$, $AC = c + F/q$, which falls as q increases but never to the level of c or MC itself. If the perfectly competitive price, p, is set below c, there can be no profits made as fixed costs cannot be covered. If p is set above c, then there is an incentive to expand supply indefinitely as an ever-decreasing price–cost margin will apply to an ever-larger output.

It also follows that efficiency requires that there be at most one producer. Otherwise there is needless replication of fixed costs, F. As a result, this situation is known as a 'natural' monopoly. Having more than one producer will definitely be inefficient although only having one will open up the prospect of monopoly power. If the price system is to be used to underpin supply, the best way to do this might in principle be to cover fixed costs F for the producer with a lump sum subsidy and charge price c to consumers. The reason is that the fixed costs have to be spent if the good is to be supplied at all. And, given this, it is best to charge consumers the marginal cost of supply, c. If a lower price is charged, then the firm would not produce unless subsidised, but this would be at the expense of alternative use of the resources going into c. If a higher price is charged, then a good could be provided at cost c, but some consumer who would only pay that amount is being denied the good at that price. With price $p = c$, the demand, using same demand curve as before, would be $D - c$ (since the demand curve is effectively $Q = q = D - p$).

Even so, leaving things to the market is not going to work. What would happen in the case of a monopoly if things were left to the market? For profit maximisation, marginal revenue is set equal to marginal cost and the latter is c. But marginal revenue is no longer equal to the prevailing price as in perfect competition. Instead, the monopolist knows that the more that is sold the lower the price must be, increasing the revenue on the extra units sold but reducing the revenue on those that could be sold at a higher price. Now, revenue $R = pq = (D - q)q$. So, differentiating for q, $MR = D - 2q$. This equals MC, c, when $D - 2q = c$, or $q = (D - c)/2$. In other words, the monopoly output is exactly half that of the efficient outcome. And, after simple manipulation, $p = (D + c)/2$ which is, unsurprisingly, bigger than the efficient price, $p = c$, as D needs to be bigger than c (see above, since D is the maximum price anyone will pay for the good). Finally, profits, Π, can be worked out as $qp - qc$ or $q(p - c)$. This is readily shown to equal $\{(D - c)/2\}^2$.

4.3 From Monopoly to Oligopoly

Now consider a situation in which there are a number of producers but there is not perfect competition, and that the price has settled at a level, p' say, where this is high enough to guarantee positive profits (to cover fixed costs, F, and unit variable costs, c) but lower than the monopoly price (at which the industry cannot secure higher profits, whether one or more producers). If a firm increases its price, it will lose all of its sales to its competitors. On the other hand, if it decreases its price it will attract all demand and, potentially, put all other competitors out of business. Accordingly, they might be expected to lower their price as well. This will either lead to a downward spiral of prices until zero profits are reached for all, or the price will settle at a reduced level and lower profits for all too. Working backwards from these outcomes to the original situation where a firm is considering changing its price from a profitable equilibrium, it follows that no firm has an incentive either to reduce or to increase price. As a result, any price between zero profit and the monopoly level potentially supports equilibrium.

This form of price competition is known as Bertrand competition. It has introduced a new element to the analysis that did not need to be present for perfect competition (when all that firms need to know is what the externally given price is) and for monopoly (when there are no other firms) – that is, firms need to take a view on what other firms are going to do in deciding what to do themselves. In the case of Bertrand competition, it is assumed that there is retaliation by other firms to a price drop by lowering their own price. So firms choose not to drop their price as the results would appear to be disastrous.

But is this necessarily so? Suppose we are in a Bertrand equilibrium over time, with each firm earning profit Π/n, year in and year out, where there are n firms and Π is annual industry profit. If a firm marginally reduces its price, it will take the entire market for one period, with other firms taking zero profit for that period, after which the initiation of intense competition will drive price down to the competitive level and zero profits for all. Each firm must choose between an income stream of Π/n for the current year and subsequently forever (should none reduce price) or Π (or a little less) for the current period followed by 0 ever after as the industry collapses into perfect competition, that is between $(\Pi/n, \Pi/n, \Pi/n, ...)$ and $(\Pi, 0, 0, ...)$. This is a choice, in present value after discounting future returns, between $\Pi/n + \Pi/nr$, and Π as the latter term in the first expression is the value of the future income stream of leaving things as they are (see Box 4.1) together with current, shared profits if price remains unchanged in the first period. So any firm has an incentive to break the collusion if $\Pi > \Pi/n + \Pi/nr$; or if, after simplifying, $(n - 1)r > 1$.

Thus, the equilibrium is more liable to be broken the larger the number of firms (because profits are being shared with many others) and if r is bigger (since the future profit stream foregone will be worth less). So the higher r is, the more likely a firm is to make an aggressive fixed investment, for example to expand capacity even though the cost of capital for investment is higher (and would suggest that investments levels would be lower).

Although Bertrand price competition gives some interesting results, the most famous model of oligopoly, the Cournot model, which like Bertrand originates from the middle of the eighteenth century, is different in two respects. First, firms compete on the basis of how much they supply, not what price to charge as for Bertrand, that is, by q not p. Second, the assumption is that there will be no retaliation by other firms to a change in own output. In other words, in the Cournot model it is presumed that each firm takes the output of other firms as

Box 4.1
What is an annuity worth?

First of all, consider a geometric progression (GP). This is something that goes up by the same multiplicative factor from one element to the next, so a, ab, ab^2, ab^3 to ab^{n-1} if there are n terms, starting with a and going up by b from one term to the next. To add this up, the a can be taken out as a common factor, and we need to focus on:

$$S = 1 + b + b^2 + b^3 + ... + b^{n-1}$$

Note that:

$$bS = b + b^2 + b^3 + ... + b^{n-1} + b^n.$$

Subtracting one from the other means:

$$S - bS = 1 - b^n$$

or $S = 1 - b^n/(1 - b)$ as long as $b \neq 1$ (as this would mean dividing by zero, and the sum of the GP would simply be nb). So the original GP sums to $a(1 - b^n)/(1 - b)$ as long as $b \neq 1$.

For a constant stream of income, or annuity, of 1 per annum starting from next year, the net present value is, for rate of interest, r:

$$1/(1 + r) + 1/(1 + r)^2 + 1/(1 + r)^3 + ...$$

For the moment, suppose the payments stop after n periods, then this is a GP with multiplicative factor $1/(1 + r)$. So, after n years, it would sum, from the formula above with both a and b equal to $1/(1 + r)$, to:

$$1/(1 + r)\{1 - 1/(1 + r)^n\}/\{1 - 1/(1 + r)\}$$

As n goes to infinity, $1/(1 + r)^n$ goes to zero and the whole expression simplifies to $1/r$.

given (there is no retaliation) in deciding how much to produce itself, bearing in mind any increase in supply will bring down the price for self and the rest of the industry (although the latter is of no consequence to the firm itself).

Formally, for the Cournot model, let there be n firms, with the ith firm supplying output q_i. And let industry supply as a whole be Q, that is, $Q = \Sigma q_i$. The ith firm takes the rest of the industry output, Q_r say, as given, where then $Q_r + q_i = Q$. As a result, the ith firm only takes variation in its own output choice as affecting its profit and so maximises:

$\Pi_i = pq_i - cq_i - F = (D - Q)q_i - cq_i - F = (D - Q_r - q_i)q_i - cq_i - F = Dq_i - Q_rq_i - q_i^2 - cq_i - F$

$d\Pi_i/dq_i = D - Q_r - 2q_i - c = 0$, when:

$q_i = (D - Q_rc)/2$ (4.1)

This is called the reaction function for the Cournot firm, telling us what the ith firm produces, given the aggregate production of other firms, Q_r.

But the extremely convenient and frequently adopted assumption will now be made – that all firms are identical. This will, as in other cases, allow equilibrium to be found most easily (although firms in competition are generally, in reality, seeking to distinguish themselves from their rivals, a point taken up below, although they might end up the same in equilibrium or as equilibrium is defined). So, for n identical firms each q_i is the same and equals q, say. And $Q_r = (n - 1)q$. From (4.1), it follows relatively simply that $q = (D - c)/(n + 1)$ and $Q = nq = n(D - c)/(n + 1)$. From substituting for Q in the demand curve, $p = (D + nc)/(n + 1)$. Π_i can be calculated as $\{(D - c)/(n + 1)\}^2$. And total industry profit is $\Pi = n\{(D - c)/(n + 1)\}^2$. You can, for example, work out the result for a duopoly in which n = 2.

Note, though, that by setting n = 1 we get the monopoly result. The need for positive profit has, however, been overlooked, and maximum profits might prove negative if F were very large, and so there would be no supply. In case F is zero, so that firms simply have costs, c, per unit of output, then there is the possibility of perfect competition, with zero profits, price p = c and output D – c. Note that as n goes to infinity, we get perfect competition, with price going to c and firm and industry profits going to zero (although this can never be realised in practice since fixed costs, F, will not be covered). This all seems to support the idea that the more the number of firms the better off the economy is (at least in partial equilibrium), since prices fall and output increases towards efficient levels as n increases.

But there is a striking anomaly in the Cournot model. Whilst each firm is identical to others, it presumes that others' output remains fixed whilst it varies its own to maximise profits. In other words, each firm both assumes that others behave differently than it does itself and is wrong in that assumption (since each firm changes its output when others do). There are essentially inconsistencies in what is called the 'conjectural variation', in how each firm assesses the way in which they believe other firms behave and the way in which other firms do behave themselves (both according to the model and the firm's knowledge of its own behaviour). Why assume other firms behave differently than yourself and persist in false beliefs about how other firms behave – as if they do not respond when you adjust your own output?

Note that this does not apply to the Bertrand model since each firm does expect other firms to behave exactly as it would itself – sit tight if others raise price but retaliate if they reduce price. Nor does it matter for finding an equilibrium, since, once there, no firm has an incentive to change and so conjectures about other firms' output, other than that it is fixed, are essentially irrelevant. But it is hardly satisfactory to have a theory that only applies in equilibrium.

A different model, which highlights rather than resolves this problem, is one way of looking at another famous model of oligopoly, the Stackelberg duopoly model which dates from the 1930s. In this case, one firm (called the leader) does take into account that the other firm (the so-called follower) is playing the Cournot game. In fixing its output, it factors in that when increasing its own output the other firm will respond by taking the new level of output of the leading firm as given. In other words, the follower firm acts as if Cournot, but the wily leader takes this into account in its own decision rather than presuming the other firm's output is fixed whatever it does itself. This gives the leader firm a greater incentive to increase its output over and above what it would do as a Cournot firm. For the latter, others' output is taken as given but, for Stackelberg, the leader reckons the other firms will reduce their output in response to its own increase in output (the opposite of retaliation) since its own higher output will already have taken demand further down the demand curve.

More formally, put aside fixed costs and use subscript F for follower and L for leader. For the follower, the situation is the same as for the Cournot firm, so that the same reaction function can be used, where $Q_r = q_L$:

$$q_F = (D - q_L - c)/2 \tag{4.2}$$

But the leader takes this reaction function into account, knowing that an increase in its own output will lead to a compensating decrease in the follower's output (by a half from inspection of the reaction function). The leader knows, in other words, that by increasing its output it will get some compensating decrease from the follower. So, in formal terms:

$$\Pi_L = (D - Q)q_L - cq_L = \{D - (D - q_L - c)/2 - q_L)\}q_L - cq_L.$$

If this is expanded and differentiated with respect to q_L, and set equal to zero and solved, it is found that: $q_L = (D - c)/2$, the same as the monopoly output. And $q_F = (D - c)/4$ from substituting for q_L in (4.2).

Total industry output $Q = 3(D - c)/4$, with $p = (D + 3c)/4$. So, in this respect, it is as if we have a Cournot outcome with three firms. But, of course, the leader makes a bigger (twice) profit than the follower since it is producing twice as much:

$$\Pi_L = (D - c)^2/8 \text{ and } \Pi_F = (D - c)^2/16.$$

Note that because this is as if a Cournot with three firms, the two firms could do better by cooperating at Cournot (if not monopoly) since total profit would be $2(D - c)^2/9$ (see formula above for Cournot for n = 2) as opposed to $\Pi_L +$ $\Pi_F = 3(D - c)^2/16$. But the Stackelberg leader gets a profit that, at $(D - c)^2/8$, is higher than the Cournot profit of $(D - c)^2/9$ whereas, of course, the follower gets a lower profit share in a lower amount of profit at $(D - c)^2/16$.

Whether a Stackelberg follower would challenge a leader or not depends on what would happen after the event. Suppose that the follower decided to try and become the leader and increases output to the same level as the leader, $(D - c)/2$. The result is that industry output jumps to $(D - c)$ and profits fall to zero for both firms (not even accounting for fixed costs, F) as this is the competitive output. Suppose after this, though, the leader and follower settle into a cosy Cournot duopoly.

If the follower had done nothing, its profit stream indefinitely would be $(D - c)^2/16$. But by challenging the leader, the profit stream is zero for one year followed by $(D - c)^2/9$ ever after (although, as well, other assumptions could be made about the impact of breaking an equilibrium and what happens subsequently). As a constant future income stream is worth $1/r$ of its annual value where r is the rate of interest, the follower will not challenge the leader where:

$$(D - c)^2/16 + (D - c)^2/16r > 0 + (D - c)^2/9r, \text{ or where}$$
$$9r + 9 > 16, \text{ or } r > 7/9.$$

That is a very high interest rate and not liable to be achieved. This means the right-hand side of the equation above is liable to be greater than the left-hand side, and the option of breaking with leader/follower is liable to be adopted. The result is hardly surprising since the follower only has to give up profits altogether for one year in order to get higher Cournot profits, $(D - c)^2/8$ instead of Stackelberg follower $(D - c)^2/9$ ever after. If it takes longer to come to a Cournot accommodation, then there is lesser incentive to break the Stackelberg as zero profits will be suffered for longer. Of course, the best outcome for the pair is to collude as a monopoly and share monopoly profits, $(D - c)^2/4$, so that they can each get $(D - c)^2/8$ forever.

4.4 A Little Game Theory

Although the Stackelberg model begins in some sense to deal with consistent conjectural variation, it worsens rather than resolves the problem since, whilst one firm takes the other's true behaviour into account (in terms of reaction function) the other does not. And if both do, they both seem to lose out, at least in the short term until an accommodation is reached. Another way of looking at the problem of conjectural variation is through game theory. In game theory, each firm, or player more generally, has a set of well-defined strategies – such as profit maximisation in the context of the theory of supply. When one strategy is taken hypothetically for each player, it gives a set of outcomes with a corresponding distribution of rewards or what are termed payoffs. A Nash equilibrium, named after the mathematician, in game theory is defined in terms of a set of strategies, one for each player, that give payoffs from which no player can be made better off by changing strategy. The Cournot model, for example, is a game in which each player maximises profits subject to the other players' outputs being taken as given. The equilibrium is given as above since, once in it, no player has an incentive to change strategy since they will become worse off by doing so. The Stackelberg model also gives a game-theoretic equilibrium, since each player cannot improve given the set of strategies available to them. This depends, however, on the asymmetrical position of the players in that they behave differently. In principle, the strategy involving the follower breaking with its defined role is not allowed. If it were allowed, then the available strategies and outcomes do need to be specified for what is effectively a different game.

There are many different games but focus here will be given to what is probably the most famous, the so-called 'prisoners' dilemma'. A crime has been committed and there are two suspects, A and B. The prosecutor wants to get a conviction for conspiracy and is prepared to be lenient if successful. If both plead guilty they will only receive a sentence of two years each. If both plead innocent, there is still sufficient evidence to be convicted of a minor offence, with each suffering five years imprisonment for frustrating the prosecutor. If A pleads guilty, and B innocent, A will be held solely responsible for a major crime and get ten years whilst B will get off altogether, and vice versa.

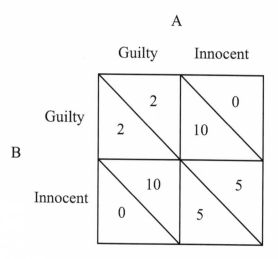

Diagram 4.2   The prisoners' dilemma

The game is represented in Diagram 4.2. Whatever A does (pleading guilty or innocent), it is better for B to plead innocent, and vice versa. As a result, the Nash equilibrium (one in which no player has an incentive to change strategy given what the others are doing) is that they both plead innocent (if A pleads innocent, B is better off doing so too since he only gets five rather than ten years; and if A pleads guilty it is also better for B to plead innocent since he gets off altogether rather than getting two years). But the equilibrium is one in which each gets five years and a better outcome for each is one in which they both plead guilty and only get two years each.

The prisoners' dilemma is that pursuit of self-interest, in this case a lower prison sentence, leads to an outcome (with both pleading innocent) in which each could do better (by both pleading guilty). In other words, the Nash equilibrium is Pareto inefficient. Further, even if they both agreed in advance with one another to plead guilty, there is no guarantee that each would keep to the bargain. Such a dilemma is hardly surprising since there are clear externalities around what the prisoners plead as the game is not zero sum (the same total prison sentence to be divided between them irrespective of outcome) with, in particular, positive sum benefits of cooperation (four years imprisonment in total as opposed to ten).

Many ways have been proposed to resolve the prisoners' dilemma. What they tend to share in common, though, is to change the nature of the game. One way is to modify the prisoners' motivations to allow for some degree of fellow feeling (for the other), but this is equivalent to changing the payoffs (since A is pained by B's sentence and vice versa). It should also be understood that self-interest as such is not the problem as is illustrated by what might be termed the siblings' dilemma (invented by me) in which each prisoner wants the other to get as light a sentence as possible without regard to own sentence. See Diagram 4.3, in which the original prisoners' dilemma has been modified slightly. In this case, each sibling pleads guilty to give the other the lower sentence, and each ends up with a higher sentence than if both had pleaded innocent.

Another way out of the dilemma is to allow for enforced cooperation, but then you are not allowing for the strategy of both pleading guilty. Sometimes this is put in terms of each prisoner needing assurance that the other will plead cooperatively. But the prisoners' dilemma is not about assurance as the only assured thing within the game is that each will plead innocent. This issue can be illustrated by reference to another game, the assurance game itself, as shown in Diagram 4.4, sometimes known as the stag hunt and deriving from Jean-Jacques Rousseau in the eighteenth century.

If both plead innocent, they both get off. If both plead guilty, they get a lower sentence of two years each. But a major sentence of ten years is given to the one who pleads guilty if the other pleads innocent, who also receives a five-year sentence by virtue of association with the guilty party. Now if both plead guilty,

A

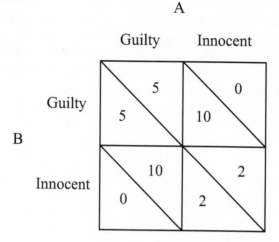

Diagram 4.3   The siblings' dilemma

A

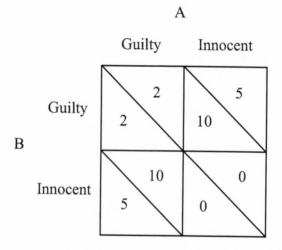

Diagram 4.4   The assurance game

neither has an incentive to plead innocent since the sentence will go from two to five years. And if both plead innocent, neither has an incentive to change since the sentence will go from zero to ten years.

In this case there are two equilibria: both plead innocent or both plead guilty, with the former a better outcome than the latter. Each prisoner needs to be assured that the other will plead innocent in order also to plead innocent and get the best outcome. But, having got to the best outcome, there is no need to enforce the cooperation as it remains guaranteed by pursuit of self-interest. So, cooperation can be a good thing but it may or may not occur through pursuit of self-interest (the assurance game) as opposed to requiring enforcement (the prisoners' dilemma) or abandonment of self-interest – a stag can be caught by cooperation but only a hare without it, with half a stag being better than a hare!

A third way to modify the game is to allow for it to be repeated. So you play the dilemma once, then again, and again, and so on. Would this make any difference to the outcome? First, bear in mind that repeated games just mean more complex strategies and outcomes. For the prisoners' dilemma, if played twice there would be four possible strategies for each player (two in each game combined with one another and so 2×2) with a corresponding set of outcomes depending on the result in each period. Played over n periods, there would be 2^n possible strategies for each player.

Would repeated games make any difference to outcomes, for the prisoners' dilemma for example? Before answering it is necessary to consider how long the game is played for, that is, how often it is repeated. If it is played over a finite time, then it is not liable to be effective in bringing about change in strategy. This can be seen by working backwards from the last period or time that the game is played. Whatever has happened before, each player is liable to plead innocent since this is the last play of the game and the best strategy is to plead innocent whatever the other player does now and whatever else has happened in the past. The same argument can then be run backwards over each of the previous periods.

If, though, the game is run indefinitely, the previous argument does not hold. Possibly, one player would plead guilty in the hope that the other would do so. But this would not work as the other could get off indefinitely by pleading innocent. However, a player could switch between pleading guilty to pleading innocent when the other player pleads innocent, and both gain a reputation for doing so and teach the other player to plead innocent as well (or get punished if not doing so). Whether this happens or not depends upon what is called the folk theorem, with outcomes contingent upon the discount rate (as future benefits and costs of reputation/learning depend on how they are valued against the present). If the rate of interest is very high, the value of future rewards will be very low and there will be no cooperative equilibrium. But if the rate of interest is low, gaining a reputation for punishing and teaching the other to cooperate can reap sufficient rewards to make it worthwhile.

In conclusion, there were great hopes (and to some extent, self-serving and persistent beliefs) that game theory would and could resolve problems around (inconsistent) conjectural variation by finding equilibria for which it is no longer a problem. In equilibrium, you no longer have to worry about how other 'players' behave as neither you nor they have an incentive to change behaviour. But, ultimately, game theory has the effect of only dealing, if at all, with the problem of conjectural variation by replacing it with what are arguably even more serious if related problems. On the one hand, as illustrated by the prisoners' dilemma, there are serious weaknesses within game theory. Most important is that outcomes are fully determined by the externally given set of strategies and corresponding outcomes. The rules and the results of the games are given and cannot be changed even if there are good reasons for players to make changes – by becoming less selfish or by bringing in enforced cooperation. Each of these two options, precluded by the game in the first instance, has been collected under the umbrella of the generic term of 'institutions', with these standing either for learned or customary behaviour beyond pursuit of self-interest or for mechanisms of enforcement, through the state for example. Otherwise, in repeated games, there are issues of for how long the game is played and whether outcomes allow for reputations and learning to be taken on board. In short, game theory points to the need to study institutions, customary behaviour, learning and so on but it is stretching the credibility of game theory to see these as reducible to a bigger, better game.

A further point is that this all depends upon everything being laid out in advance (strategies and payoffs) for all players with perfect knowledge of others' options, extended over time. Game theory itself indicates that even within these background assumptions, according to which model is deployed, there is enormous variety in the sorts of solutions that can be attained. Necessarily, such variety can only be intensified if there is deviation from these assumptions.

Place this once more in the context of conjectural variation. The results from game theory, if not equilibrium within a particular game itself, suggest that this cannot be ignored; that players have to take a view about what other players' views are in order to be able to form their own. What game does each think the other is playing? What reputation do I hold of them and vice versa? What have they learned and is it correct? What 'institutions' and customary behaviour (in pursuit or even in lieu of self-interest) are in place? Are there multiple equilibria? And so on. Such questions undermine the idea that the way to proceed is to take individual behaviour as given by pursuit of self-interest and the strategies and outcomes available, and then work out optimal strategies. This is because, even if motivation can be taken to be one-dimensional in terms of profit or utility maximisation, even defining what that is or how to pursue it for the individual is interdependent with the motivation and behaviour of others. At the grand theoretical level, this means that possibly the most important implication of game theory is that it is essential to begin, not with the optimising individual, but with the social conditions and context in which that individual is located. How do these factors condition cooperation, collusion, conflict, etc., with these being incapable of reduction to previously formed and exogenously given individuals alone?

Significantly, such conclusions were in many ways unwittingly adopted by those studying competition in analyses preceding the emergence of game theory, possibly as part of what for them was common sense. Behaviour could be based upon what appeared to be plausible behavioural assumptions, such as Cournot, Stackelberg or Bertrand, that might be more or less realistic in one context as opposed to another. Such an approach reflected an inductive, institutionalist approach to competition. The more the extent of monopoly, the closer an industry is liable to be monopoly pricing. So let the price–cost ratio be higher, the more concentrated is an industry. To some degree, game theory, together with the wish to underpin non-competitive markets to the calculations of optimising individuals, represented an explicit attack upon what were perceived to be arbitrary assumptions (even though they might prove to be broadly correct in appropriate circumstances). The non-competitive mark-up ought, for example, to be the consequence of optimising behaviour, not some random rule.

Well, now we know better. The results from game theory suggest that it is impossible for players to know what game they are playing, let alone what game other players are playing, what strategies they are adopting, and so on, even though their own strategies need to take a view on this. In this light, it does make some sense to restore behavioural models as a simple fix in analysing non-competitive behaviour, just as firms in real life have to make judgements and act upon them, rather than resolve the conundrums presented by both conjectural variation and game theory.

4.5 A Simple Model of Entry Deterrence

So far, in departing from perfect competition with free entry and exit of firms, the emphasis has been upon competition in the form of price (Bertrand) or quantity (Cournot/Stackelberg) variation on the part of a given number of firms within the industry. But now suppose that there is no longer perfect competition in entry and exit as well; that these are not costless – you have fixed costs to enter that you do not fully recoup if you exit. In particular, consider a monopolist or so-called incumbent that is under threat of entry from another firm. If the cost of entry is zero (what is called perfect contestability, see Box 4.2) then there is liable to be entry, as profits are to be made and entry will be made by other firms too, so that the industry is liable to move to perfect competition.

Suppose that there is a fixed cost of entry, F, with a corresponding annual interest payment (or cost of entry), rF, where r is the rate of interest. Before a firm decides to enter or not, it has to take a view on what the post-entry outcome is liable to be. Suppose, for example, that it is taken to be Stackelberg, with the entrant being the follower and the incumbent being the leader. Then, after entry, the entrant's annual profit will be $(D - c)^2/16$ (see Section 4.3). If rF is greater than this, the incumbent's monopoly is secure.

Does this mean that there will be entry if $rF < (D - c)^2/16$? Not necessarily. The incumbent could deliberately set a higher output than the monopoly level

---

Box 4.2
Contestability

As has been seen, if there are increasing returns to scale, perfect competition in the sense of every firm being a price-taker (sell as much as you like at a given price without bringing the price down), cannot work. Either no profits can be made if the price is set below the lowest possible average cost, or profits and output will be expanded indefinitely if there is a price-cost margin at all. This is easy to see if there are fixed costs, F, and unit variable costs, c, with the results contingent on whether p is greater or lesser than c. No profits are possible if $c = p$ (since it is not possible to cover fixed costs, F), or $c > p$ (it is not possible to cover fixed or variable costs) and infinite profits are possible if $p > c$ as F will soon be swamped by growing profits as output increases. For the last case, output cannot expand indefinitely in practice because there would not be the demand (this was only an assumption from given price).

So what would happen in the absence of perfect competition? Suppose there is a monopoly, would it not charge a monopoly price with monopoly profits? Not necessarily: if price exceeds $F/q + c$ where q is market demand at that price, there will be positive profits. But then other firms would enter and drive down the price, albeit at the expense of temporary inefficiency (see Section 4.5). So the only equilibrium is if the monopoly charges the price $F/q + c$. Paradoxically, then, there will be both a monopoly and no monopoly profits (these would be eroded by entry by other firms). It is indicative that increasing returns to scale (so-called natural monopoly) and presence of a monopoly does not mean that there is no competition. This is so if entry and exit is costless, i.e. $F = 0$. Whilst there might not appear to be competition because of the monopoly, there is said to be (perfect) contestability. Interestingly, the theory of contestability was used to justify deregulating airlines under Reagan's neoliberal presidency, possibly on the grounds that anyone can hire an aeroplane and run a service. Note that exit costs also have to be zero for perfect contestability, so that entering firms will not make a loss on their fixed costs once they leave the industry again after grabbing surplus profits. It is a moot point whether fixed costs in the airline industry are minimal or that they lead to a 'race to the bottom', or deteriorating standards as a result of fierce cost and price competition (think bucket shop airlines).

---

in order to reduce price and dissuade the entrant from entering. It may be worth the incumbent doing this rather than sharing the market with the entrant. What the incumbent has to do is work out what level of its own output would just discourage the entrant from entering. It then has to compare the profit from this with the alternative of allowing entry and taking Stackelberg leader profits. If the latter is bigger, but it might not be, it is better just to allow the entrant in.

From the Stackelberg model (see Section 4.3) the entrant's profits would work out to be $(D - q_I - c)^2/4$, where subscript I is for incumbent. So the point at which the incumbent can prevent entry is where $(D - q_I - c)^2/4 = rF$. For convenience let $rF = A^2$. This means allowing entry or not around $(D - q_I - c)/2$

= A; or where $q_I = D - c - 2A$. In other words, a slightly higher output than this will keep a potential entrant out.

At this output, $p = c + 2A$ and $\Pi_L = (D - c - 2A)2A$. So this is the profit that the incumbent makes if it keeps the entrant out. Otherwise, it makes the Stackelberg leader profit of $(D - c)^2/16$. Depending on which of these two is bigger, the incumbent allows entry or not. The tipping point is given by:

$$(D - c - 2A)2A = (D - c)^2/16.$$

This is a quadratic equation in the variable A. It can be easily shown that it has the only sensible solution:

$$A = (D - c)(2 - \sqrt{2})/8.$$

Or, what turns out to be $rF = A^2 = (D - c)^2(3 - \sqrt{2})/32$ after squaring and simplifying. With $\sqrt{2}$ approximately equal to 1.4, and $3 - \sqrt{2}$ approximately equal to 1.6, this is around $0.8(D - c)^2/16$. Recall from earlier, there is no entry if $rF > (D - c)^2/16$ since the entrant's follower profits do not pay entry costs.

Therefore, below $rF = 0.8(D - c)^2/16$, incumbent allows entry. With rF above $(D - c)^2/16$, the entrant does not want to enter in any case. But, in between these two values, the incumbent supplies a level of entry-deterrent output above the monopoly output (and price below monopoly price) just sufficient to keep the entrant out (see Diagram 4.5).

Values of rF for:

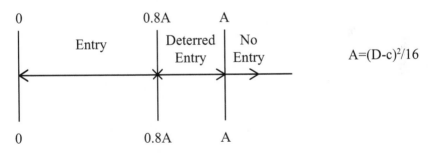

Diagram 4.5   Deterred entry, or not?

4.6 Collusion

Because of the problems of individual, competitive optimising in the presence of interdependencies (and conjectural variation) but absence of perfect competition, there has within microeconomics been some support for restoring a degree of behavioural assumptions in the context of oligopoly. Rather than seeking to resolve the inconsistencies and conundrums involved in conjectural variation, why not adopt more or less rules of thumb for how firms might behave and incorporate them theoretically? It might be assumed, for example, that firms price by adding a fixed mark-up on costs. This would, though, raise the questions of how the mark-up is chosen and what happens if different firms adopt different mark-ups with corresponding differences in demand or market share, let alone competitive survival.

This issue of price discrimination is taken up later. For the moment, observe that a fixed mark-up on costs would gain a definite rule for pricing, subject to costs having been predetermined, but at the expense of abandoning any conjectures about other firms' behaviour or response. Models of collusion proceed differently. Firms could get together, fix prices, and share output amongst themselves. Ideally, for them if not consumers, a cartel would be formed which maximised profit as if it were a monopolist, produced corresponding output across firms at minimum cost, and shared the profits of doing so in an agreed fashion. Even so, each individual producer might well have an incentive to break the cartel (as if in a prisoners' dilemma, see Section 4.4).

Whether they do so or not will depend upon how other firms might (be perceived to) retaliate. If this is thought to be a correspondingly high increase in output, there will be lower profits for all, and this might deter an attempt to profit from being in breach of the cartel. There may not even be a formal agreement at all, and just the threat or fear of retaliation may be enough to induce firms to restrain themselves in what is termed tacit collusion.

Such tacit collusion will be modelled below. First, though, let us return to the case of a monopoly producer with profit Π, demand curve $p = D(q)$, and cost curve $C(q)$:

$$\Pi = pq - C(q) = qD(q) - C(q).$$

This is maximised for:

$$d\Pi/dq = qD'(q) + D(q) - C'(q) = 0.$$

This is so when:

$$\{D(q) - C'(q)\}/D(q) = -qD'(q)/D(q) \tag{4.3}$$

Recalling that $D(q) = p$, and $D'(q) = dp/dq$, and marginal cost, $MC = C'(q)$, this means that:

$$(p - MC)/p = -\{qdp/dq\}/p = -1/(p/q) \, dq/dp.$$

Now the left-hand side here is the percentage increase of price over MC. For competitive equilibrium, p = MC. So the right-hand side can be interpreted to be a measure of what is termed the (percentage) degree of monopoly in the sector. The right-hand side of the equation is simply the inverse of the elasticity of demand for the good, e say (see Box 4.3). It follows that for a monopoly, the degree of monopoly equals 1/e.

Note that this is infinite if e = 0. This is because demand is fixed irrespective of price. A monopolist would increase price indefinitely and decrease output towards zero without loss of demand. At the other extreme, where e = ∞, p = MC, and demand is perfectly elastic or as if perfectly competitive (increase price and lose all your market, decrease price and get as much as you want). It also follows that necessarily e > 1 for an optimising monopolist who will move to a point where demand is elastic. If e < 1, output can be reduced and revenue increased. This is because by increasing price and reducing output sold, revenue will be increased (a percentage fall in output is less than a percentage increase in price) and, as a bonus, there will be lower costs incurred on lower output, unambiguously increasing profits on revenue and costs. Interestingly, somewhat perversely given its popularity, for a Cobb–Douglas utility function from which demand curves have constant elasticity of demand equal to one (q = $\alpha I/p$, where I is income and α the shared exponent in the utility function for q at price p), there is no possibility of monopoly since output will be set at zero and price infinitely high. For these properties of the Cobb–Douglas utility function (see Box 4.4).

The monopoly case serves as a standard against which to assess collusive oligopoly. Now consider a number of firms, n, with notation as before but with typical firm indexed by i, for i running from 1 to n, the number of firms. The ith firm maximises:

$$\Pi_i = q_i D(q) - C_i(q_i),$$

where $q = \Sigma q_i$ equals sector output as a whole across the n firms.

When i maximises profit, account must be taken of its own increase in output and how this affects both overall demand D(q) and individual firms costs $C_i(q_i)$:

$$d\Pi_i/dq_i = D(q) + q_i dD/dq_i - C_i'(q_i) \tag{4.4}$$

For the Cournot model or, indeed, the monopolist (as there is only one producer) dD/dq_i, how much price changes because q_i is increased only depends upon q_i itself, with q_j for j ≠ i taken as given and unchanging. But if there is anticipated retaliation for q_i of increased output as punishment from other firms, j, i has to make some conjecture over what it is going to be.

Box 4.3
Elasticities

An elasticity, not surprisingly, measures how flexible or elastic something is. But to make it change, something else must also change to create the effect. But to compare elasticities, of different flexibilities of different things in response to different prompts, it is necessary to scale the measurements. Otherwise, for example, measuring a change in centimetres would give one-hundredth the elasticity of measuring it in metres. The simplest way to handle this is to measure elasticity by the percentage change in one thing relative to the percentage change in another (and bear in mind that the order in which this is done inverts the elasticity and does not have any implications for causation). As long as the things can be measured, their changes relative to one another can be expressed as elasticities: percentage change of splurge relative to percentage change in gobbledygook for example. Note that elasticities are dimensionless because they are the ratio of one dimensionless quantity (a percentage) relative to another.

In economics, it is commonplace to work with elasticities at the margin, so that the quantity response to a price change becomes $(dq/q)/(dp/p)$ or $(dq/dp)(p/q)$ for price, p, and quantity, q. With an own price elasticity of demand, that is liable to be negative, the convention is to change the sign to make the elasticity positive. Note that revenue $R = pq$ so that $dR/dp = pdq/dp + q$.

So $dR/dp \geq 0$ as $pdq/dp + q \geq 0$ or $(dq/dp)(p/q) + 1 \geq 0$ or $e = -(dq/dp)(p/q) \leq 1$ where e is elasticity of q relative to p.

It follows that revenue increases with price if $e < 1$ and decreases if $e > 1$, and constant for $e = 1$ (for which percentage decrease in quantity impacts on revenue equal and opposite to increase in revenue for increase in price as $R = pq$). This is hardly surprising since when e is inelastic (less than one) when you increase price, quantity changes less than in proportion and so more than sustains the level of revenue, and vice versa when e is elastic (greater than one).

Finally, suppose that $q = Ap^e$ for some constants A and e. Leaving aside signs, it then follows easily enough that e will be the elasticity of q relative to p. So if q is proportional to p, this is equivalent to the elasticity being equal to one. Also take logs, then:

$$\ln q = \ln A + e\ln p.$$

What this tells us is that if we have a linear equation in logs, then the coefficients – just one in this case, e – are the elasticities of the dependent relative, q, to the independent variable, p. More generally, then, if:

$$q = \ln A_0 + \alpha_1 \ln p_1 + \alpha_2 \ln p_2 + \dots + \alpha_n \ln p_n.$$

This is equivalent to a Cobb–Douglas functional form (see Box 4.4), with elasticity of q relative to p_i equal to α_i, the latter itself the exponent in the Cobb–Douglas function on p_i.

Box 4.4
The Cobb–Douglas functional form

The Cobb–Douglas utility function for two goods, x and y, may be written as $u = x_1^\alpha x_2^\beta$ for parameters α and β, the exponents on x_1 and x_2. More generally than for utility alone, e.g. for production functions too, this is known as the Cobb–Douglas functional form. For $\alpha + \beta = 1$, there are constant returns to scale. Note, though, that if we squared or cubed the utility function (or subjected it to any positive function), it would make no difference to the indifference curve; they would simply be relabelled with different numbers. Getting to a higher indifference curve would appear to give more utility, but this is just scaling – in the same way that temperature is hotter or colder and only fixed on a scale (centigrade or Fahrenheit) by convention. The same is not true of production functions and isoquants, as these represent definite magnitudes of inputs and outputs, not relative measures or, more exactly, orderings of utility.

For the Cobb–Douglas utility function, by maximising utility, it is readily seen, because relative marginal utilities equal relative prices, p_1 and p_2, that:

$$p_1/p_2 = \alpha x_1^{\alpha-1} x_2^{\beta} / \beta\, x_1^{\alpha} x_2^{\beta-1} = \alpha x_2 / \beta\, x_1.$$

Since the ratio of the quantities is proportional to ratio of the prices, it immediately follows that the elasticity of substitution is constant and equal to 1 (see Box 4.5 on elasticity of substitution).

It can also be shown relatively easily, by solving the first order conditions for utility maximisation, that the (Marshallian) demand curve for x_1 is given by:

$$x_1 = \alpha I / p_1 (\alpha + \beta), \text{ where I is income.}$$

And, by symmetry, $x_2 = \beta I / p_2 (\alpha + \beta)$. It follows that $p_1 x_1 / I = \alpha/(\alpha + \beta)$ and $p_2 x_2 / I = \beta/(\alpha + \beta)$. In other words, the share of consumer expenditure for the Cobb–Douglas utility function for any good is equal to its share in the exponents, $\alpha/(\alpha + \beta)$ and $\beta/(\alpha + \beta)$, which necessarily sum to 1. It also follows from the demand functions that own price elasticity (percentage change in demand for percentage change in price) is 1 and cross-price elasticities (the change in demand because the price of the other good changes) are 0 (this must mean income and substitution effects always just cancel each other exactly). Finally, income elasticity for demand for each good is simply equal to 1.

These results are so commonplace, and the Cobb–Douglas functional form is used so much, that it is worth students tattooing the results on their foreheads so that they can be recalled if forgotten and not be a source of puzzlement when used without explanation. But it is also worth emphasising how special are the assumptions necessary for Cobb–Douglas, with so many elasticities fixed at very special constant values for all levels and patterns of consumption.

Box 4.5
Elasticity of substitution

In case of an indifference curve, and an optimising consumer, relative marginal utilities are set equal to relative prices. Suppose relative prices change – in favour of one good and against another – then there is substitution from one to the other along a given indifference curve. But just how much substitution is there? Do consumers only change a little for a big relative price change or do they change a lot even for a small change? These questions are answered by defining the elasticity of substitution which, in principle, could be different at each and every point of consumption. If there are two goods, x and y, with prices, p and q, then the elasticity of substitution is defined as the elasticity of y/x relative to q/p. Given $p/q = u_x/u_y$ for utility function u(x,y), this is a complicated expression in general terms but can be represented relatively easily in graphical form as the percentage change in the ray from the origin to the point of consumption for a change in the tangent to the indifference curve (see Diagram 4.6).

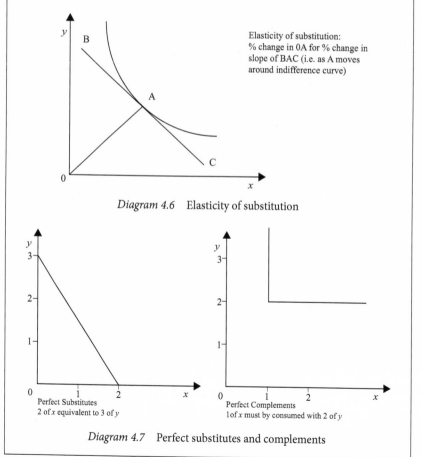

Elasticity of substitution:
% change in 0A for % change in slope of BAC (i.e. as A moves around indifference curve)

Diagram 4.6   Elasticity of substitution

Perfect Substitutes
2 of x equivalent to 3 of y

Perfect Complements
1 of x must by consumed with 2 of y

Diagram 4.7   Perfect substitutes and complements

There are two neat special cases. One is where the indifference curves are straight lines, as in Diagram 4.7. In this case, there is perfect substitutability between the two goods and you switch completely from one to the other according to which is relatively cheaper. A price line will take you to one or the other axis, unless it is parallel or coincides with the straight line indifference income, in which case it does not matter in what proportions the two goods are consumed as they are both essentially the same and are priced the same. The other extreme is perfect complements, i.e. no substitutability at all, where indifference curves are right angles. In this case, you have to consume the two goods in fixed proportions and so any change in relative prices makes no difference to your patterns of consumption between them.

As $p = D(q_1 + q_2 + ... + q_n)$:

$$dD/dq_i = D'(q)(dq_1/dq_i + dq_2/dq_i + ... + dq_n/dq_i) \tag{4.5}$$

with each of the terms in the last bracket representing the anticipated change in supply by firms in response to change in q_i.

Previously, dq_j/dq_i (for Cournot, and monopoly), was taken to be zero for $j \neq i$, and necessarily 1 for $j = i$. Now, otherwise, it is necessary to decide upon what value is taken by dq_j/dq_i when it is not zero as for Cournot.

Just assume, somewhat arbitrarily, that other firms, j, react to i by increasing their output towards maintaining their pre-existing market share. If doing this exactly, $dq_j/dq_i = q_j/q_i$, such would be perfect retaliation as far as market share is concerned since ratios of supply would remain the same. But a more moderate response would be to increase output only in some proportion, α, between 0 and 1. If it is assumed that $\alpha = 0$, this will be Cournot, but for $\alpha = 1$, as will be seen later, the outcome is equivalent to monopoly. More generally, for any α: $dq_j/dq_i = \alpha q_j/q_i$ when $j \neq i$ and, of course, $dq_i/dq_i = 1$.

This means that the *industry* response dq to *firm* change dq_i, since $q = \sum_{j=1,n} q_j$, is given by:

$$dq/dq_i = 1 + \sum_{j\neq i} dq_j/dq_i = 1 + \sum_{j\neq i}\alpha q_j/q_i = 1 + \alpha \sum_{j\neq i} q_j/q_i = 1 + \alpha(q - q_i)/q_i.$$

So, from (4.5):

$$dD/dq_i = D'(q)\{1 + \alpha(q - q_i)/q_i\}.$$

And, so, from (4.4):

$$dΠ_i/dq_i = D(q) + D'(q)\{q_i + \alpha(q - q_i)\} - C_i'(q_i) = D(q) + D'(q)\{(1 - \alpha)q_i + \alpha q\} - C_i'(q_i) \tag{4.6}$$

With some manipulation, this equals zero for profit maximisation when:

$$\{D(q) - C'_i(q_i)\}/D(q) = -\{(1 - \alpha)q_i/q + \alpha\}qD'(q)/D(q).$$

Looking back to (4.3), this is a revised formula for the degree of monopoly, $1/e$, if for the individual firm, i, rather than for the single monopoly firm, since $D(q) = p$ and $C'_i(q_i) = MC_i$. It equals $\{(1 - \alpha)q_i/q + \alpha\}/e$. Note that for $q_i = q$ (or one firm), this is equivalent to monopoly as is $\alpha = 1$ (anticipated retaliation to sustain market share).

But what about the degree of monopoly for the industry as a whole, across all the firms taken together? This might be *measured* (emphasis will be explained later) by adding up over individual firm degrees of monopoly. But what if one firm has a large market share and a large degree of monopoly (not fanciful as will be seen)? A simple average of the firms' degrees of monopolies would under-represent the extent of price over marginal cost for the sector as a whole. So, it makes sense to take a weighted average of the degrees of monopolies. If weighted by market share, the sectoral degree of monopoly would be given by:

$$\Sigma\{(1 - \alpha)q_i/q + \alpha\}q_i/eq = \{(1 - \alpha)/e\}\Sigma q_i^2/q^2 + (\alpha/e)\Sigma q_i/q = \{(1 - \alpha)/e\}H + \alpha/e,$$

since for the second term in the middle expression, $\Sigma q_i/q = 1$; and, for the first term, H is known as the Herfindahl index (after its inventor, see Box 4.6).

Ultimately, then, for the sector, the degree of monopoly, contingent upon level of concentration and degree of collusion, equals $\{(1 - \alpha)H + \alpha\}/e$. There is perfect monopoly, $1/e$, in case $H = 1$ or $\alpha = 1$.

Box 4.6
The Herfindahl index

The Herfindahl index is a general statistical measure of concentration or inequality. In the application here, there are n firms, each with market share q_i/q, with this necessarily reflecting the random chance you would buy the good from firm i if you bought it just once. By the same token, q_i^2/q^2 is the probability that, if you buy the good twice, you will buy it both times from i. It follows that $H = \Sigma q_i^2/q^2$ measures the overall probability that if you bought the good twice, you would have bought it from the same firm on each of the two occasions, whether from i or one of the other firms. Note that for monopoly, or one firm taking all output, $H = 1$. And, for equal shares, $q_i = 1/n$, so that $H = n \times 1/n^2 = 1/n$. This is the smallest value of H for n firms. And so H varies between $1/n$, its smallest value, and 1; that is between perfect equality across all firms to perfect inequality (one firm with everything), respectively.

Previously, it was signalled that this is a *measure* and, by implication, not a *determination* of the degree of monopoly. What does this mean and why is it important? Well, if an industry is observed with given values of α, H and e (although it is not clear how we would know α), the degree of monopoly can be calculated from the formula. But this does not explain why these values prevail. Even if α and e are fixed as some sort of exogenous parameters, H is endogenous, determined within the model itself by the individual values of firm outputs, q_i, from which it is calculated. The firm outputs, q_i, take on values that can in principle be determined from the n equations and the n unknowns given by setting formula (4.6) equal to zero for each i, equations which, themselves, ultimately depend upon the demand function, D, and the cost functions, C_i.

These equations, though, can only (begin to) be solved in practice once the cost functions are specified. To this end, take a very simple form for these. Suppose each $C_i(q_i) = F_i + c_i q_i$. This is our old friend with fixed costs, F_i, and unit variable costs, c_i, although these are allowed to vary across firms (and so equilibrium will not be the same for each firm). It might be expected that F_i and c_i would be inversely related. This is because by laying out higher fixed costs you might be able to save on unit variable costs. Some firms may, though, have higher F and c, even though they are less efficient in both respects than other firms. But if the collusive price is high enough to allow for profits, even those that are inefficient will get some market share. More efficient firms will allow the price to be high enough to allow in the inefficient since they gain more from the higher prices than they would from higher demand at lower prices (that they can in principle match with their lower costs).

With these assumptions, and going back to the profit-maximising equation for the ith firm (4.6), it follows that:

$$D(q) + D'(q)\{(1 - \alpha)q_j + \alpha q\} = C_i'(q_i) = c_i \text{ by assumption} \qquad (4.7)$$

Adding over all such equations for the n firms:

$$nD(q) + D'(q) \{(1 - \alpha)q + n\alpha q\} = \Sigma c_i$$

or

$$nD(q) + D'(q) \{(1 - \alpha)q + n\alpha q\} = \Sigma c_i.$$

Divide through by n and let $\Sigma c_i/n = c$, the average marginal cost across all firms, then:

$$D(q) + D'(q)\{(1 - \alpha)q/n + \alpha q\} = c.$$

Now, subtract this equation from (4.7) for the individual firm, i, and the result is:

$$D'(q)(1 - \alpha)(q_i - q/n) = c - c_i.$$

This is a neat, even remarkable result, possibly appearing otherwise until the expression at the beginning of the right-hand side of the equation, $D'(q)(1 - \alpha)$, is ignored as merely some sort of scaling. Recall that c is average unit variable cost and q/n is average output. What the equation reveals is that each firm's output, q_i, will deviate from the average firms' output in proportion but in the opposite direction as the deviation of its unit variable costs, c_i, from the average of these across the industry. In other words, the more unit variable cost, c_i, is smaller (bigger) than the average, the bigger (smaller) is its allocated output, q_i, in proportion.

So the firms with the lower unit variable costs will enjoy a higher level of output. This would appear to be admirable as costs will tend to be lower given overall level of output (and given all firms' fixed costs have to be covered). Nonetheless, the good news is laced with bad news. For, whatever the overall level of output, it would be better for it all to be produced by the firm with the lowest unit variable costs. At least this would bring costs to a minimum. The firm with the lowest unit variable costs could even bribe the other firms not to produce at all and pay them the profit they could otherwise expect plus some share of the cost savings! Effectively, this would be a monopoly with its rewards distributed to others. In its absence, the potential, single, most cost-effective producer charges a price that allows others to supply even if tacitly colluding in a way that provides for its larger market share (its price–cost margin, or degree of monopoly, is larger as is the output supplied upon it).

Interestingly, the theory of the degree of monopoly was developed by Michał Kalecki, and it has strong overtones with what is known as the monopoly capital, underconsumptionist school associated with the US Marxists, Paul Baran and Paul Sweezy. Here, the argument is that the greater the degree of monopoly (and collusion), the higher the price level and the lower the output and the less the level of real wages. The result is stagnation at the macroeconomic level as lower real wages confront higher prices and restricted output and employment.

The results presented here suggest a different interpretation of how to understand competition and monopoly, not within the model itself but through the implications for competition that it does not include. First and foremost, as demonstrated, those firms that have higher unit variable costs, and a correspondingly lower degree of monopoly, output and profits, have an incentive to reduce their variable unit costs. How can they do this? As hinted at earlier, the answer might well be by expanding fixed costs, F. This aspect of competition has been excluded from the model.

Also excluded is entry into the sector, as n is fixed, and this again is a different form of (excluded) competition (and recall from the deterrence model that prices may have to be reduced to keep entrants out). Competitive entry could lead to more investment and not stagnation. Also, entry could be by acquisition or merger to close down less efficient firms – again another, excluded form of competition. Nor is any account taken of what is known as countervailing power. Not all production is for final consumption to atomised workers as consumers with no market power. Intermediate products may be purchased by equally monopolistic producers that use their market power to resist unduly highly priced inputs.

In short, in working from within the model for implications for what it excludes, it is found that much that is part and parcel of competition is vital without being taken into account: cost competition through investment for higher market share and price–cost margin; entry, acquisition and mergers; and, it should be added, competition for market share across sectors on the demand side. It is to these that the discussion now turns.

4.7 Discriminating Models

As suggested, firms do not only compete by price. Another way in which they compete is by discriminating themselves from others in various ways, in seeking out consumers and profits (advertising being the most obvious example to highlight real or imaginary differences between products in the minds of potential purchasers). A neat model of competition suggested by Hotelling concerns ice cream sellers on a straight line beach of given length who discriminate between themselves by where they locate their stall. The best place for a single seller to position to maximise sales is in the middle of the beach to minimise the overall inconvenience of holidaymakers, evenly distributed across the beach, covering the distance to get their ice cream. However, a second seller would get less than half sales (as holidaymakers travel to the nearer seller), unless positioning exactly adjacent to the first in the middle of the beach (so that those to the right of them buy from one, and those to the left buy from the other). So the competitive result is for there to be two sellers, back-to-back in the middle of the beach. This is inefficient since overall inconvenience would be reduced if the sellers were further apart (overall inconvenience, and maximum sales, is suited by having each of two sellers one-quarter of the way from the end of the beach at opposite ends, and no one has to walk more than a quarter of the beach). Note that if one positions in the ideal position, the other will go just the other side to serve three-quarters of the beach. Then the other will do the same and so on until both are at the centre again. This is like the prisoners' dilemma in which, whatever one does, it is better for the other to go to the long side, so the only equilibrium is the inefficient one (in which both lose as both could get more custom if they took and stayed at the ideal positions – since they would share a larger clientele, including those at the beach's extremes who would otherwise not be bothered to take the long walk for an ice cream).

This might explain why there is often so little product differentiation by qualities, other than location, even when there are lots of sellers. Each is going for the bulk market. But the opposite can occur with artificial or real proliferation of differences between products in order to create a local monopoly for profits. The simplest way in which this is done is through price itself. Other than in the world of perfect competition, increasing your price a little will not necessarily lead you to lose all of your demand, as with convenience stores for example.

Consider the following model developed by John Sutton and then by Richard Schmalensee. The idea behind this model is that, whilst there is a natural monopoly and the economy is best off with a single producer selling at unit variable cost once fixed costs are covered, price competition will allow firms to enter the market until profits are driven down to zero. For a given number of firms, each has to decide what price to charge to compete with the others. If competition is fierce (reduce your price a bit and you get a lot of the market), prices will be low as will be profits, as they are driven down by the threat of firms entering to take advantage of the profits to be made. This is like the contestability discussed in Box 4.2. What the model seeks to do is to find out how the equilibrium price level and number of firms varies as market size, fixed costs and strength of competition vary. It makes sense to suspect that the number of firms, for example, will increase with market size relative to fixed costs and with increased competitiveness.

To make matters simple, the model will focus upon the competition alone (as opposed to collusion) by only allowing for a fixed level of overall demand S (taken as exogenous although how outcomes vary with S as a parameter will be examined later). This means that firms compete for market share but not at the expense of overall demand that remains unaffected by their pricing. Suppose the ith firm's market share is given by $[p_i^{-e}/\Sigma p_j^{-e}]$ where p is price and e is a positive parameter larger than zero. This looks complicated, but basically it is saying that each firm's own price elasticity is e but it is necessary to scale this by the Σ term to make the sum of the market shares add up to one. If e goes to infinity, then price responsiveness is very elastic and firms must all charge the same price to retain any of the market share. On the other hand, if e = 0 then each gets the same market share, $1/n$. However, it turns out that e must be bigger than 1, otherwise firms will increase their price and not lose enough market share to undermine the profits of higher price (a bit like the monopolist always being on the elastic part of the demand curve).

The ith firm chooses p_i to maximise: $\Pi_i = (p_i - c)S(p_i^{-e}/\Sigma p_j^{-e}) - F_i$, where F_i are fixed costs. Let Σ stand for $_{j=1,n}\Sigma p_j^{-e}$ and Σ' for $_{j\neq i}\Sigma p_j^{-e}$. Then:

$$\Pi_i = (p_i - c)S(1 - \Sigma'/\Sigma)$$
$$d\Pi_i/dp_i = S(1 - \Sigma'/\Sigma) + Se(p_i - c)\, p_i^{-e-1}\Sigma'/\Sigma^2.$$

This is a bit of a mess. But it is possible to make a simplifying assumption that can be justified and allows for the algebra to be relatively easily resolved. This is that familiar assumption that all firms are or turn out to be the same. Why, after all, would they be different, at least in equilibrium? This is a bit perverse because the whole object of the exercise is to study firms that discriminate amongst themselves by price, only they end up being the same. This is because there is no way within the model to distinguish one from another, and they are only using price to compete, and all compete in the same way and end up the same. So, in equilibrium, all firms have common price p and, from the equation above, $d\Pi_i/dp_i = 0$ when, after dividing throughout by S:

$$1 - (n - 1)/n - e(p - c)(n - 1)/n^2 p = 0$$

since $\Sigma' = (n - 1)p^{-e}$ and $\Sigma = np^{-e}$, as all p_js are the same.
Simplifying further, this gives:

$$np - e(p - c)(n - 1) = 0$$

and $p(n - en + e) + ec(n - 1) = 0$ or:

$$p = ec(n - 1)/(en - e - n)$$

How does this compare with unit variable cost, $p - c$? $p - c = ec(n - 1)/(en - e - n) - c$ which, when simplified, equals $nc/(en - e - n)$.
    Each firm has market share S/n, so profits per firm are $Sc/(en - e - n) - F$.
    Suppose now that firms enter (or exit) until profits are zero in what might be thought of as long-run equilibrium in which a previously exogenously given number of firms, n, is now determined as n^*, that is, $F = Sc/(en^* - e - n^*)$. From this we can solve for n^* and find that:

$$n^*F(e - 1) = Sc + cF.$$

It follows that for the long-run number of firms, with perfect entry/exit in case of non-zero profits:

$$n^* = (Sc/F + e)/(e - 1) \qquad (4.8)$$

For the latter, long-run price is given by: $(p^* - c)S/n^* = F$, so that fixed costs are just covered by market share S/n^*. It follows that:

$$p^* = c + Fn^*/S = c + F(Sc/F + e)/(e - 1)S.$$

This simplifies to:

$$p^* = e(Sc/F + 1)/(e - 1)S/F.$$

Note that as e gets very big – market share responds very much to price decrease – then the formula for n^* goes down towards one (4.8). And the price, p^*, falls towards $c + F/S$ (this is easiest to see from the penultimate equation with n^* going towards one). This is an ideal outcome. Paradoxically in a way, competition for market share is so fiercely responsive to price that price is driven down such that only a monopoly can cover unit and fixed costs, with market demand, S, covered by a single firm with single fixed costs, F. Despite monopoly, higher price would invite competitive entry for market share. Sutton suggests this might be a commodity like salt that attracts no customer loyalty so that, whilst you get a monopoly, prices are kept low by threat of competitive entry.

But as e gets down towards one there is limited competition for market share, so unresponsive is it to price, and the number of firms is much larger. Each firm can be more or less guaranteed to retain its market share. So plenty enter, raising the number of fixed costs that have to be covered, and also raising prices indefinitely. This is where customer loyalty is strong in the face of price increase.

Also note that as S/F (the size of the market relative to the fixed costs) gets very large, the number of firms, n^*, increases indefinitely too. And, as S/F rises, the price tends towards $ec/(e - 1)$. If e is large, this goes down towards c, hardly surprising as there is lots of competition with low fixed costs. Otherwise, even with large numbers of firms, there is a premium, $e/(e - 1) - 1$ or $1/(e - 1)$, on unit variable costs to cover fixed costs of those large numbers of firms.

A second model considered by Sutton/Schmalensee is one in which firms compete by cost with similar assumptions made for fixed costs, F, and overall market size, S, although in this case price p is taken as given, and firms can vary c_i to get a larger market share. This might be interpreted as a higher unit variable cost to improve the quality of the product even if sold at the same fixed market price, p. In other words, all the producers charge the same price but each can get higher market share by raising the unit variable costs they put into the product. It might be fancy packaging or it might be better ingredients. The modelling strategy will be as before. Formally, the ith firm's profit is given by:

$$\Pi_i = (p - c_i)S[c_i^e/\Sigma c_j^e] - F.$$

The same exercise can address profit maximisation, by varying c_i for the ith firm. This can then be solved by setting each c_i equal to one another (all firms the same) to find optimal cost, c, for a given number of firms, n. Then long-run number of firms, n^*, can be found for free entry/exit and with profit set equal to zero. Fortunately, it is unnecessary to go through the mathematics again, as it has already been done. Simply set p to −c and vice versa, S to S, e to −e, and F to F, and this becomes the problem just done. Accordingly, using this symmetry from before with '$p = ec(n − 1)/(en − e − n)$', then:

$$-c = ep(n − 1)/(-en + e − n) \text{ or } c = ep(n − 1)/(en + n − e).$$

For, '$p − c = nc/(en − e − n)$', it follows that:

$$p − c = -np/(-en + e − n) = np/(en + n − e).$$

From '$n^* = (Sc/F + e)/(e − 1)$':

$$n^* = (− Sp/F − e)/(− e − 1) = (Sp/F + e)/(e + 1),$$

and for '$p^* = e(Sc/F + 1)/(e − 1)S/F$', it follows that:

$$c^* = -e(-Sp/F + 1)/(-e − 1)S/F = e(Sp/F − 1)/(e + 1)S/F.$$

Not surprisingly, there are similar results for our extreme values. Remember that price is fixed and firms can vary, that is, increase c, to get larger market share. For e increasing indefinitely, n^* goes to 1, and c^* to $(Sp/F − 1)/S/F = p − F/S$. The latter means that competition is so fierce there is just one firm with costs driven down to spread fixed costs, F, over the market, S. On the other hand, with e being driven down towards zero – it makes no economic sense for e to go down to −1 in parallel to lower limit of +1 for e for the previous parallel case – then n^* becomes Sp/F and $c^* = 0$. In other words, the number of firms fills out the market just sufficiently to cover fixed costs at given price – each firm produced S/n, at price p with fixed costs F. Also, as S/F increases so does n^*, and c^* goes towards $ep/(e + 1)$ or $p = (e + 1)c^*/e$ with a premium of 1/e on unit variable to cover fixed costs.

A final model in this vein allows for competition for market share through changing fixed costs, A_i, for the ith firm, say. This might be motivated by the idea of fixed advertising costs, A, on top of fixed production costs, F, or overhead costs might genuinely enhance quality. In this case, with fixed price, p, and unit variable costs, c, the ith firm maximises:

$$\Pi_i = (p − c)S[A_i^e/\Sigma A_j^e] − A_i − F.$$

Using similar Σ notation as before:

$$\Pi_i = (p − c)S[1 − \Sigma'/\Sigma] − A_i − F.$$

This is maximised for A_i when:

$$(p - c)S[eA_i^{e-1}\Sigma'/\Sigma^2] - 1 = 0.$$

And, using once more the assumption that all firms are identical and so each A_i will be the same, A say. Then:

$$S(p - c)e(n - 1)A^{e-1}A^e/n^2A^{2e} - 1 = 0 \text{ or } (p - c)e(n - 1) = n^2A.$$

This means that as n goes to infinity, A goes to zero. Firms do not compete with one another by advertising if there are lots of them. And as e goes to infinity so does A, since the more rewards there are the more firms will advertise. But with such numbers of firms and levels of advertising there is no guarantee of positive profits as a binding constraint. If, once again, free entry and exit is allowed, apart from expenditure, F, then the no profit condition is:

$$(p - c)S/n^* = A^* + F \text{ or } A^* = (p - c)S/n^* - F \qquad (4.9)$$

This means A^* and n^* are inversely related for zero profit (irrespective of the optimisation condition).

Combining this with the previous equation to eliminate A^* gives:

$$S(p - c)e(n^* - 1) = n^{*2}\{(p - c)S/n - F\}.$$

This gives the following quadratic equation for n^*:

$$(F/S)n^{*2} + (p - c)(e - 1)n^* - e(p - c) = 0.$$

This only has one (sensible) positive solution. But what happens as S/F goes to infinity? The first term in the last equation goes to zero and n^* tends towards $e/(e - 1)$, a definite limit. This means that as market size increase indefinitely, relative to fixed costs, the number of firms does not increase. Instead, a limited number of firms, at most $e/(e - 1)$, respond to increasing market size by competing with one another through unlimited additional fixed expenditure, A, with $A^* + F$ tending towards $(p - c)S(e - 1)/e$ (which increases indefinitely with S), as can be seen from (4.9) since n^* tends towards $e/(e - 1)$. On the other hand, if e goes towards infinity the first term becomes negligible relative to the others, and n^* tends to 1. This also means that $A + F$ tends to $(p - c)S$. In other words, there is a monopoly and the single firm deploys the entire margin of (fixed) price over cost (and fixed costs) to spend on advertising, thereby retaining full market share but making no profit in deterring entry. If advertising works well, then, even as market size increases indefinitely a single firm will use the extra revenue to spend on advertising to retain market share.

4.8 Path Dependence

Path dependence is a generic term, far from unique to economics or economic history, indicating that subsequent outcomes in some process are contingent on how you got where you are as well as where you are. Just to make the point clear in an economics context, general equilibrium is not path dependent given that outcomes only depend on your endowments, technologies and preferences (as well as perfect competition, independently optimising agents, etc.). Of course, being at a place in motion is different from being there at rest as it might take you time to get going at full speed. But this is not path dependence proper, since your speed now is part of where you are at now. Path dependence would also require that your speed or something else in the past is relevant and continues to exert an influence over your future over and above getting you to where you are now.

A common example of path dependence within physics is hysteresis, with a spring for example. Pull it apart and it springs back, and so there is no apparent path dependence. But pull it too far and it does not spring back fully and there is path dependence. Applying a magnet (or electro-magnetic field) to materials is similar. When the magnetic field is taken away some, such as iron, retain their magnetism (path dependence) and some, such as steel, do not. The same sort of path dependence has been suggested for the long-term unemployed in macroeconomics (albeit on microeconomic foundations). Those individuals who remain out of work or the job market for a long time may lose their motivation for, and skills within, work and increase what is presumed to be the natural rate of unemployment. In other words, long periods of unemployment in the recent past mean that macroeconomic equilibrium, or trade-offs between unemployment and other policy goals such as inflation, take place at higher levels of path-dependent unemployment. Stretch unemployment too far, and it may not spring back to former levels when economic conditions improve.

However, within economics the most prominent field of application of path dependence has been technological change, underpinned by the idea that once one technological trajectory has been taken it becomes hard to shift to another because it is embedded in other historically previous developments that will also have to change simultaneously or sequentially, whether economically efficient to do so or not. An obvious example is the huge difficulty shifting from private cars to public transport for example (let alone from other environmentally damaging technologies). In this respect, it is readily seen that path dependence does depend upon technology but also the institutions, vested interests and customs that have been built up over time. However, the most famous example of path dependence is QWERTY (see Box 4.7).

Box 4.7
QWERTY as path dependence

QWERTY is the most prominent example of path dependence and is associated with the economic historian Paul David, although an earlier example he used was the fragmented patterns of agricultural landownership in England which he saw as impeding the adoption of mechanical harvesters. With a nudge if necessary, QWERTY should be familiar to you as the order of the top left-hand row of letters on your keyboard (but not your mobile phone or other such devices). How did this come about and why does it persist? The answers given by David, although they are disputed especially by those, usually neoliberals, who wish to minimise the significance of path dependence, are as follows. First, in the days of mechanical, manual typewriters, when long-armed keys were made to move by pressing the keys, an arrangement of the keys was made in order to minimise the chances, with fast typing, that two keys would collide and jam (one on the way up and the other on the way down to striking the paper with a ribbon in-between key and paper). It made sense to keep keys apart that were likely to be commonly used together. This arrangement of the keys certainly did not coincide with alphabetical order.

Second, with the displacement of the manual typewriter by separate mechanical printing from word processors, the jamming problem no longer prevailed. Note that it did potentially continue with the first electrical typewriter, which used motors rather than the hands' force to move keys, but even this was no longer a problem with IBM's golf ball (which had the symbols arranged around a sphere which was moved electrically to type without danger of jamming – this invention put IBM on the map although it has long since disappeared and is only remembered by the generation that used it, as it was soon taken over by word processors). However, despite the confinement of QWERTY to the dustbin of technology, it still persists on keyboards, other than mobile phones etc., but even there when the keyboard is displayed more fully. The reason is, of course, that everyone has already learned to use the QWERTY keyboard in their touch-typing or otherwise. To change would impose a cost on unlearning the old keyboard and learning whatever was standardised as the new. There would also have to be some degree of replacing or modifying existing keyboards.

Consequently, it seems as if we are locked in to the old QWERTY technology. It is a moot point whether this is because it would be inefficient to change, and/or too arduous to organise. But in this, as in all other supposed examples of path dependence, it is crucial to see whose interests are served or not by the change as well as who might or might not have the power and motivation to bring it about, and under what circumstances.

It is relatively easy to offer a simple model of the costs and benefits of switching or not. Should an economy persist with a given technology, for which fixed costs, F_1, have already been laid out, or introduce a new technology with fixed costs, F_2, that would have to be incurred. Suppose that unit variable costs for the two technologies are c_1 and c_2, with $c_1 > c_2$, possibly justifying a switch to the new technology. Then annual fixed costs for introducing the new costs are $F_2 r$ for interest rate, r. If market size is S, then it is worth switching if $(c_1 - c_2)S > F_2 r$, as saved unit variable costs would exceed extra fixed costs. Clearly this is more likely, the bigger are $(c_1 - c_2)$ or S (that is, the extra unit cost on the old technology or larger market size) or smaller are F_2 or r (smaller interest costs on capital expenditure). Of course, if the choice between the two techniques could be made before F_1 has been laid out, the second would be chosen if:

$$Sc_1 + F_1 r > Sc_2 + F_2 r \text{ or } (c_1 - c_2)S > (F_2 - F_1)r.$$

Not surprisingly, this is a weaker condition than before (since no account is taken of fixed costs, F_1, already incurred).

It might seem strange to include consideration of path dependence in a chapter on competition. But the previous discussion has been about the choice of technology for the economy as a whole. This might not involve a single firm and, as a result, the fixed costs, F_2, of switching might be those that need to be incurred across a group of producers (and/or consumers). An example for the latter in my own lifetime, if probably not yours, was the switch to natural gas in the UK for which the nationalised gas industry took on the cost of converting every household appliance that had previously relied upon gas produced from coal. More likely in your own experience, has been the shift from analogue to digital TV signals for which consumers were required to purchase, rather than provided for free with, a 'set-top box' to allow compatibility with old equipment.

However, when firms are competing with one another, the situation may be more complex. If all currently use the old technology and all have access to the new, say more efficient, technology, then the problem of switching to the new may be an assurance problem (see Section 4.4 on game theory). Everything is OK as long as all switch together with, for example, a common move to a new standard that is interchangeable across products and producers. On the other hand, there could be a prisoners' dilemma situation in which, whatever the other producers do in committing to share in covering the costs for a new standard or not, it is better to free-ride by imposing the costs of change on others. None pays, and so there is no change even though it would be better for all if everyone paid. Some enforcement mechanism may be necessary.

Even if all firms are the same in terms of access to both old and new technology, there may be a need for some non-market solution to bring about technological change when it is warranted by cost considerations, either to coordinate firms or to coerce them. The situation is even more complicated when firms are not identical in their access to the old and new technologies. An incumbent using the old technology may be resistant to change to the new technology for fear of losing markets and monopoly position, and adopt a competitive strategy to impede adoption of the new technology that may be more readily available to others – just as an incumbent in general may seek to deter competition from entrants.

Here a relationship between path dependence and competition is revealed. This has, for example, been prominent in the challenges made to Microsoft's competitive behaviour in which the notion of path dependence has been used in court cases in defence of what might be claimed to be its anti-competitive behaviour. Before explaining why, consider the relationship between *economies of scale* and *economies of scope.*

Economies of scale are already familiar; the idea is that productivity is higher, and unit costs lower, the more is produced. As seen already, a simple example of economies of scale is with fixed costs, F, and unit variable costs, c, with output S sharing the fixed costs. Economies of scope prevail where there are gains to be made in productivity by producing two different things at the same time. As a simple algebraic example, suppose one good can be produced with fixed costs, F_1, and unit variable costs, c_1, and similarly for the second good, with F_2 and c_2, but that with a single fixed cost, F, each of the goods can be produced with unit variable costs, d_1 and d_2, respectively. For market sizes, S_1 and S_2, costs of production for using the separate processes are:

$$S_1c_1 + F_1r + S_2c_2 + F_2r.$$

And costs for using the single process with potential economies of scope are:

$$S_1d_1 + S_2d_2 + Fr.$$

Making use of economies of scope is worthwhile when:

$$S_1c_1 + F_1r + S_2c_2 + F_2r > S_1d_1 + S_2d_2 + Fr, \text{ or}$$
$$S_1(c_1 - d_1) + S_2(c_2 - d_2) > (F - F_1 - F_2)r.$$

This is more complicated than the expression for switching from one technology to another. Judgement depends upon whether higher unit variable costs are outweighed by lower fixed costs of the joint as opposed to the single technologies, or vice versa. This will also depend upon market size with, for example, larger markets tending to favour economies of scope if it has lower unit variable costs.

This is all very well in principle but what about in practice? Will a shift take place if it is economic to do so? This is where Microsoft is relevant. As far as basic software is concerned, it has established a very strong, if not exclusive presence for basic software (at least for PCs). But new applications for new software are arising all the time. Those offered by Microsoft have the advantage of economies of scope but have the potential disadvantage of poorer technology, given innovation by others, and do not necessarily enjoy economies of scale within particular applications.

For Microsoft to accrue its economies of scope, it can argue that it needs users to be aware of the benefits of, and so to choose to work with, both its basic software and its applications. Customers need to learn this, leading Microsoft to offer the application at a discount. Microsoft might even insist in its marketing that access to its basic software depends upon taking its applications as well, so that customers cannot get the second without the first. Rivals with economies of scale in the operation of the application will argue that this is uncompetitive behaviour putting them at a disadvantage.

Basically, there are two issues here. One is the question of whether economies of scale or economies of scope should prevail. This depends upon the variables listed above, around the Fs, the cs and the Ss. These might be known to the firms themselves but not to others. And some fixed costs may have been incurred in the past in anticipation of rewards. Nor are these variables fixed and certain, with market size increasing over time but also possibly under threat of erosion from further innovation. In short, it is relatively easy in simple theory to specify the relative merits of economies of scale and economies of scope, but in practice it is very difficult to know.

This is related to the second issue: the consequential interpretation of competitive behaviour. Take Microsoft for example. To accrue economies of scope across consumers, it makes competitive sense to subsidise applications. On the other hand, this is exactly the same behaviour that would be adopted if the economies of scale in basic software were being used to exploit the market for applications. In short, the more general point is that the same firm behaviour can be compatible with opposite extremes in competitiveness. But this ought to have been known beforehand as, for example, a uniform price across a large numbers of suppliers (think of numbers of market stalls selling the same thing) could either reflect perfect competition (increase price and you lose all market) or perfect collusion.

4.9 The Coase 'Theorem'

Ronald Coase received a Nobel Prize for Economics, essentially for two simple contributions (with much joking about taxi drivers knowing these things and economists bemoaning why they didn't think of them). One questioned why firms exist, with hierarchies of control within them. His answer rests on the idea of transaction costs. It can be more costly or arduous to transact through the market than simply telling somebody to do something directly. Think about the consequences, for example, if any time we wanted someone to do something for us, or provide something, we had to find or make a market and pay a corresponding price (so a 'firm' seems to be anything that takes place outside the market and might be thought to be stretched too far in scope).

Coase's second contribution also draws on the implications of the presence of transaction costs, that these are not zero as presumed in the perfect competition model attached to TA². His concern is with externalities and why these are not satisfactorily dealt with through the market. Essentially his answer, subsequently graced with the moniker theorem by others, is that if transaction costs are zero *and* property rights are assigned fully for all relevant factors of production and consumption, then the market will deal satisfactorily with externalities. Thus, for example, in case of (absence of) pollution, if it can be bought and sold freely and costlessly, then an appropriate Pareto efficient balance will be ground out through the market mechanism (with whoever owns the right to pollute being paid for not doing so to the extent that those affected are willing to pay).

Significantly, Coase himself was well aware of the limitations, even emptiness, of his so-called theorem. Essentially, in the real world, transaction costs are not zero and property rights are not fully assigned to everything, so the force of his result is little more than: if the market works well and fully, then it works well and fully. Coase's motivation was twofold: first to highlight the significance of transaction costs and property rights in practice; and, second, to criticise the notion that the presence of externalities (or public goods such as a lighthouse) justified state intervention to correct market imperfections. Rather, he argued that alternative solutions in terms of assigning property rights and relying upon corresponding private markets should be considered in practical terms, by comparison with what he dismissed as blackboard economics in which mathematical solutions were provided for a benevolent state implementing ideal policies, to eliminate externalities or provide public goods, without due regard to who gained from these policies and how well they might be implemented. Despite Coase's theorem being misinterpreted as favouring the market as opposed to Coase's own predilection for empirical investigation of the nature and incidence of transaction costs and property rights, he is not entirely blameless for this misinterpretation, given his neoliberal disposition towards favouring the market, and private property, over the state.

There are many criticisms to be made of Coase and his theorem. Most important is the failure to deal with issues of power, privilege and, in the limit, possibly (the threat of) violence as the form they take (the ultimate in transaction 'costs'). Such factors are crucial in establishing what property rights are and who owns them. You might enjoy slapping my face, but should you be assigned the property right to do so in order that I can Pareto efficiently buy it back from you? This is in part a distributional issue – it might be considered fairer for me to own slapping rights to my face and sell them to you if I wish as opposed to buying them from you. But more is involved than this, not least the historical processes by which property rights are obtained and exercised. Thus, for example, slavery constitutes an entirely different form and distribution of property rights than capitalism, and this has little to do with the incidence of, and economising on, transaction costs (although there are arguments that slavery ended to economise on raising and disciplining slaves). Such oversights are the consequences of seeking a universal, ahistorical and asocial approach to the economy – one to which, usually in addition to TA^2, is added the notion that the workings of the market are tempered by the incidence of transaction costs. And again, like TA^2 and its foundations for economics imperialism, having taken out the historical and the social to establish that transaction costs, and how they are handled, are decisive, the historical and social are brought back in to explain what was excluded. This is especially true in the new institutional economics, in which institutions are seen as a way in which the non-market makes allowances, however well, for non-zero transaction costs. But, if institutions depend on transaction costs, how did we get these in the first place, as they are not and cannot be institutionless?

This digression into the Coase theorem seems to have become tangential to the main purpose of this chapter. As with path dependency previously, what has it got to do with competition? Well, if transaction costs are zero, the presumption must be that competition is perfect. Otherwise, wherever there are positive profits, competitive entry will occur. Returning to software, suppose Microsoft appears to be exercising a monopoly, either with its operating system or applications, then this can only be because there are transaction costs to switching to other operating systems or to separately sourced applications that are not worth bearing.

What, though, of the need for coordination and cooperation to switch from a locked-in, path-dependent technology to another that is superior and worth the switch, something that would appear to require non-market coordination? Well, of course, with zero transaction costs some firm can find a way to do this by itself, or cooperation and coordination can be costlessly discovered and implemented. Why only assume market transaction costs are zero, why not assume it for all sorts of transacting? By doing so and allowing for negotiating through the market or otherwise, then society will always be able to find the best outcome across (zero transaction cost) market and non-market outcomes.

In a sense, this is a super-Coase theorem. If transaction costs are universally zero, through the market or otherwise (but if they are zero in the market, we can get anything we want in any case at zero transaction cost), then there is no reason to believe that the world is not an ideal place if left to itself. Such is the ultimate ideological rationale for neoliberalism although, in practice, it is generally laced with a heavy dose of authoritarianism (we have ways of making markets and society work – the visible hand of neoliberalism!). This is hardly surprising once recalling that zero transaction costs mean not only no need for resources to exchange but also as much time as you like in which to do it (as time is money). So, given a costless and timeless process, we really ought to be able to put everything exactly as we want it and as it should be (although, it should be acknowledged, there is a different neo-Austrian rationale for neoliberalism that favours the market for its coordination in the presence of extreme individual uncertainty and invention, as opposed to searching out an ideal equilibrium).

As indicated, such a *reductio ad absurdum* to zero transaction costs motivated Coase himself to suggest close examination of those property rights and transaction costs that exist in practice. This is, however, simply to accept uncritically that these factors should be the building blocks of economics, with or without various aspects of the technical apparatus and technical architecture of microeconomics (TA^2), as opposed to questions of power and how it is exercised. Put another way, is it appropriate to see the differences between capitalism and slavery by virtue of different arrangement of property rights in light of the different corresponding incidence of transaction costs?

4.10 Towards Alternatives

Putting this grand historical question aside, reliance upon transaction costs as an explanatory device *within* capitalism may seem more compelling. By the same token, should competition be seen, at least in part, in terms of the pursuit of lower transaction costs? This does seem to have the advantage of acknowledging that markets do not work perfectly because of non-zero transaction costs.

But, as seen throughout this chapter and even without reference to transaction costs, competition has a huge variety of factors and mechanisms at its disposal – by price, quantity, quality, discrimination more generally, productivity, collusion, economies of scale and scope, entry and exit, acquisition and merger, and so on. And outcomes in the competitive process within each of these alone are often uncertain as much in reality as with the model adopted. As a result, it is hardly surprising that there can be little consensus, either theoretically or empirically, over simple relations between degree of competition, however it might be defined, and number of firms or other variables. This is especially so because, as revealed, presence of monopoly might be subject to perfect contestability whereas a common price across many firms might be indicative of either strong competition or, alternatively, equally strong collusion to fix price.

In short, appeal to transaction costs (and property rights) as decisive in addressing competitive processes and outcomes is liable to be inadequate when stacked against a multitude of other factors that might be highlighted, such as economies of scale and scope, mergers and acquisitions, productivity increase and product differentiation. The variety and complexity of factors involved in competitive struggles suggest that any general theory will be inadequate and reductionist. This is not a recipe for abandoning theory altogether, but it does involve acknowledging that theory must leave empirical outcomes open or contingent.

In this respect, a good starting point is to allow for economies of scale. For Adam Smith, for example, productivity is driven by economies of scale, not least through his famous example of the pin factory. It involves a division of labour across tasks between workers (in the apparent absence of bosses) as a source of productivity increase (and hence competitiveness). Workers could be assigned to particular parts of the production process, such as straightening and stretching the wire, cutting the lengths, adding the point and knob at top and bottom, and also provide for the adoption of tools and machinery suitable for these tasks and economise on the equipment by dedicating parts of it to particular workers (rather than all workers making their own pins with their own equipment). Smith acknowledged that the downside of such developments promoting the wealth of nations was to deskill workers by assigning them single monotonous tasks. For Smith, then, the competitive process involved a growing division of labour to accrue economies of scale, although he also argued that such developments would eventually stagnate as markets became exhausted.

Marx, however, takes a much more wide-ranging view than Smith, whom he saw as unduly emphasising the division of labour *within* the factory, crucial though it is, at the expense of what he termed the social division of labour by virtue of commodity production as allocated *between* factories or places of work. In a sense, Marx is pointing to the interaction between economies of scale and economies of scope. He observes that the competitive process could either lead to combination of separate into single trades (Fordist mass motor car production is the archetype, with raw inputs at one end of the factory and final products at the other end) as opposed to the separation of what might have previously been combined trades (as with increasing fragmentation and subcontracting of production and reliance upon manufactured components bought in from elsewhere). Marx suggests that capitalism proceeds on the basis of one or other of these routes across time, place and sector, but theory itself is unable to determine which route will prevail – and, historically, economies have successively witnessed swings between conglomeration and unbundling.

The latter, for example, has been particularly prominent over the most recent period with the rise of 'financialisation', asset stripping and the short-term maximisation of shareholder value. Significantly, for Marx, access to finance is a major factor in the competitive process, not least in providing the capital necessary to pursue economies of scale and/or scope and in tiding over periods of recession. In general, large capitals are liable to beat out small capitals competitively. Interestingly, what was previously one of the most prominent analyses of American capitalism derived from the corporate economic historian, Alfred D. Chandler. His emphasis was placed upon what he termed the 'visible hand' of major US conglomerates and how they institutionalised the management of economies of scale and scope through a divisional management structure. How large corporations emerge and prosper is a key element in the competitive process, as has been observed in two rather different literatures: one concerned with the role of the (development) state, with the rise to prominence of Japanese *zaibatsu* and South Korean *chaebol*; and the other concerned with the role of multinational corporations in which production, trade and finance are organised across national boundaries if within firms (possibly more international trade in manufacturing takes place within corporations between their affiliates in global production networks than between different corporations or to independent consumers of final products).

Nonetheless, economies of scale and scope fit extremely uncomfortably within mainstream economics, even in a partial equilibrium context where there is a multiplicity of potential models and corresponding diversity of potential outcomes. In a general equilibrium setting, this raises questions over how prices are determined or what sort of value theory the mainstream has to offer (marginal utility and productivity meets increasing returns to scale and scope?). Price can no longer reflect a unique, stable, Pareto efficient outcome. This reflects a more general problem of how value is determined whilst technology is changing, let alone remaining the same albeit in the context of scale and scope economies. The mainstream tends to hold the economy fixed, determine prices, then allow technology to change, and move to a new equilibrium where prices emerge once more at their, admittedly temporary, equilibrium values. Alternatively, productivity is allowed to increase smoothly over time and can be factored in as a discount on saving and investment. Otherwise, attention to the price mechanism in the context of unevenly changing technology, across time, place and sector, is neatly sidestepped by assuming the presence of a single sector, or a good that serves both consumption and production in all respects, most likely with constant returns to scale and subject to smooth productivity increase over time. This gives rise to the aggregate economy as if competition and (relative) pricing is absent (and/or presumed to be perfect) (see Chapter 5).

Interestingly, Smith does attempt to address this issue: how are prices formed as productivity increases (presumably according to growing pin-factory-like division of labour)? This is surely a germane issue in today's world of electronic goods with which current levels of quality and productivity of the latest devices are obsolescent almost as soon as they hit the market, together with the prices they command. Smith's answer to the question of how prices are formed when there is growing division of labour is more significant for being posed than for the flawed answer he provides (by allowing wages and profits to be determined independently of one another whereas they must sum to net output, even if it is growing, in the absence of taking account of other rewards such as interest and rent).

The details of what is termed Smith's components theory of value need not detain us other than to observe that Marx offers a more coherent approach, in suggesting that those sectors that most drive productivity will attract disproportionately higher prices in light of their higher capital intensity (this is known in Marxist literature as the transformation problem, although it is often misinterpreted as an equilibrium theory of prices for static technology as opposed to how prices are formed as productivity increases). But more important for Marx than the level at which prices are formed are the processes by which the different aspects of competition are, or are not, coordinated through the market mechanism. For Marx, competition in pursuit of profitability through the accumulation of capital and increased productivity inevitably creates tensions that cannot always be accommodated by the market mechanism, even though these tensions might be tempered or revealed by other forms of competition than productivity increase itself (squeezing down wages or input prices, for example, or seeking protected markets). But this is no more than a summary of how Marx addresses competition within a grander vision of capitalism's structures, relations, processes and agents and how these evolve and feed into the economy's competitive dynamic.

4.11 Further Thoughts and Readings

I have covered the Kaleckian approach to degree of monopoly in Fine and Murfin (1984a, 1984b) and the Sutton/Schmalensee models of competition in Fine (1996, 1999). For discussion of Coase, his theorem, transactions costs and property rights, see Bertrand (2010), Medema (2011), and Meramveliotakis and Milonakis (2011, 2013). Wiener (2011) offers the telling argument that if society can get it together to negotiate property rights, they can surely also agree sufficiently to use resources together in common without the need for property rights as the indirect mechanism for doing so. Possibly this suggests that property rights were forcibly imposed. Smith's theory of value in light of his approach to the division of labour can be found in Fine (1982), and Marx's theory of value and understanding of technical change is addressed in Fine and Saad-Filho (2010).

5
Production Function Rules, Not OK

5.1 Overview

The purpose of this chapter is to subject the aggregate, or one-sector, production function to critical appraisal. It has been heavily used in theoretical and empirical work by the mainstream, not least in treating the supply side of the economy as if it could be reasonably represented by a simple function such as F(K, L), with this itself forming the basis not only for assessing sources of growth in output but also distributional outcomes (determination of profit and wage rates by their marginal products). This is all covered in Section 5.2. In Sections 5.3 and 5.4, the sorry tale of the aggregate production function is taken further in terms of its putative use for measuring technical change. Even on the rarefied assumptions on which this exercise is undertaken, the whole process is shown to be flawed, even incoherent.

Perversely, these results have long been accepted by the mainstream itself in principle, albeit with considerable resistance. But, in practice, the discipline continues to proceed as if they did not exist or were of limited relevance, entirely without justification even from within its own methodology and theory. This is despite, or even because of, what is shown in Section 5.5 to be an impoverished understanding both of production and technical change from a number of different perspectives. Further, although the use of production functions is unambiguously microeconomic in analytical content and is, indeed, applied at levels other than the economy as a whole (across a sector or even for individual firms), the discussion of aggregate production functions, and their application to growth theory and measuring technical change, is usually thought to be part of macroeconomics. Even here, it is often overlooked as macroeconomics is mainly focused upon short-term deviations around given long-term trends and technologies (see counterpart volume, *Macroeconomics: A Critical Companion*). Thus, presentation and critique of production functions sits equally comfortably, and uncomfortably, with microeconomics and macroeconomics. But, technically at least, it is microeconomics par excellence, however much it may have been imposed upon a correspondingly impoverished macroeconomics. And this justifies its inclusion here.

5.2 The Aggravating Aggregate Production Function

As already demonstrated, microeconomics in general is heavily centred on the technical apparatus and technical architecture of microeconomics (TA^2) both as core theory and as the corresponding basis for application to a wider set of topics than (individual) supply and demand through the market. Such are the consequences of the historical logic of economics imperialism given the universal nature of the concepts attached to TA^2. As also observed, there is a paradox, if not an inconsistency, in using TA^2 to examine those factors that have previously either been taken for granted as exogenous or, at the extreme, totally disregarded in deriving TA^2 itself. For example, TA^2 depends on the absence of externalities. But, if there are externalities, it can be argued that it does not make sense to take preferences (and utility functions) as given since individuals may choose or be induced to think differently about themselves and the world in which they live when confronted by externalities. It may encourage regard for others. As we have seen, similar issues arise in the context of competition, where conjectural variation suggests that treating (aggregate) supply as comprised of independent and independently motivated profit-maximisers is severely limited.

The reason for this tension between the derivation and the application of TA^2 comes from the sacrifices taken in the derivation – methodologically, conceptually, theoretically and with limited regard for correspondence with empirical realities (and own individual experience and forms of behaviour). Having sinned in these respects, as it were on the grandest of scales, further sins, whether large or small, seem more or less acceptable within the framing of TA^2. Thus, whilst TA^2 is fundamentally concerned with the coordination of independent optimising economic agents, utility functions for consumers, and production functions for supply, it is but a short step for these functions to become deployed as representative of the economy as a whole. This crudely sidesteps aggregation problems since such representative utility or production functions are only justifiable under the most restrictive conditions, and essentially contradict the formal results that TA^2 itself suggests, in parallel with the unacceptably strong conditions for the existence, stability, uniqueness and Pareto efficiency of general equilibrium.

These points are particularly well illustrated by the use of a production function to represent supply for some economic aggregate, ranging across a firm through a sector to the national economy as a whole, if not on a grander scale still. We know this is invalid, but we do it anyway and forget it is invalid the more we do so. As a result, it has become commonplace to represent an 'economy' by a production function, $f(K, L)$, where K is capital, L is labour and, further, the capital good that makes up K is exactly the same as the output that is then either allocated to augment K (as investment putting aside depreciation) or to serve consumption (with this single good, with no hint of irony, called putty, jelly or Meccano as, being total malleable, it can be turned to any purpose across production and consumption – maybe today's term would be Lego).

Initially, the aggregate production function was used by Cobb and Douglas to explain relative shares of capital and labour. If – hold your breath – we assume the economy can be represented by a constant returns production function, $Y = F(K, L)$, so that technological possibilities are fixed and represented by F, that there is full employment, and input and output markets are perfectly competitive, with r the rate of profit, return on capital, or rate of interest all treated as interchangeable as the cost of capital, and w the wage, then, maximising profit, $\Pi = f(K, L) - rK - wL$ gives:

$$d\Pi/dK = F_K - r = 0; \text{ and } d\Pi/dL = F_L - w = 0,$$

i.e. the marginal product of capital (labour) equals its price, r (w).

The share of profits in national income equals $rK/F = KF_K/F$ and the share of wages equals LF_L/F. With constant returns to scale, by what is known as Euler's theorem, these two shares do add up to 1 (see Box 5.1). Moreover, if the production function is Cobb–Douglas, $F(K, L) = AK^\alpha L^{1-\alpha}$ where A is a constant, then $rK/Y = \alpha$ and $wL/Y = 1 - \alpha$. In other words, factor (profit and wage) shares are constant.

If the assumption of the Cobb–Douglas production function (what is called the functional form) is added to all the other assumptions, then it is predicted that factor shares will be constant. Significantly, in the 1930s, when the Cobb–Douglas production function was first prominently proposed, factor shares were considered to be relatively constant. Since then, of course, they have tended to swing in favour of labour in the post-war boom, and the other way under neoliberalism. This lay in the future but, even so and unfortunately, the presumption of constant factor shares was perceived to offer empirical support and legitimacy for utilising production functions in general and a Cobb–Douglas in particular.

This is totally fallacious. In the first place, it involves discussion of the empirical evidence supporting something that it is known cannot be true (given the other assumptions necessary for the production function to prevail). Second, it confuses a necessary with a sufficient condition, as if because a donkey has a tail all animals with a tail must be a donkey. For the Cobb–Douglas, for example, $AK^\alpha L^{1-\alpha}$, and so, for small changes in inputs:

$$dY = A\alpha K^{\alpha-1}L^{1-\alpha}dK + A(1 - \alpha)K^\alpha L^{-\alpha}dL.$$

Divide through by $Y = AK^\alpha L^{1-\alpha}$ and:

$$dY/Y = \alpha dK/K + (1 - \alpha)dL/L \tag{5.1}$$

Box 5.1
Returns to scale

A production function, with two variables say, can be expressed as $Y = F(K, L)$, where Y is output, K is capital and L is labour. By returns to scale is meant how much output increases when each of the inputs is increased in the same proportion. If for all values of K and L, for example, increasing inputs by a certain factor, such as doubling, always doubles output, then there are said to be constant returns to scale. Formally, for scaling inputs by t:

$Y = F(tK, tL) = tF(K, L)$ for constant returns.

More generally, if output more than increases in proportion to inputs there are said to be increasing returns to scale, and decreasing returns if output less than increases. Note that there are always increasing, constant or decreasing returns for a particular initial level of inputs and proportional change in these. But, in general, there is no reason why a particular production function should exhibit the same returns for each initial set of inputs and their increase in proportion. So systematic returns across all initial input choices is a special property – the production function $KL + K + L$ for example does not have systematic returns. This would require that the isoquants always remain the same shape, with the returns measured by increasing, constant or decreasing depending on how much output increases as you move from one isoquant to another further out representing the use of more inputs in proportion.

If there are such systematic returns always in the same proportion, whether constant or not, then a more general formula, or property, for scale returns is, for any t, that: $Y = F(tK, tL) = t^\lambda F(K, L)$ with $\lambda = 1$ for constant returns, $\lambda > 1$ for increasing returns, and $\lambda < 1$ for decreasing returns.

In these cases, the (production) function is said to be homogeneous of degree λ. If so, note that the isoquants will always be of exactly the same shape as one another in terms of their curvature. So, know one, and you know them all. This is known as being homothetic. To fix them exactly quantitatively, it is also necessary to know what is happening to output in moving between these isoquants. Of course, the degree of homogeneity could change rather than be constant whilst the production function retained the property of being homothetic.

For a homogeneous production function, differentiate the previous equation for t, to give:

$KF_K(tK, tL) + LF_l(tK, tL) = \lambda t^{\lambda-1} F(K, L).$

Set $t = 1$ and this becomes $KF_K + LF_l = \lambda F$. This is known as Euler's theorem. Given F_K and F_L are marginal products of capital and labour, respectively, then KF_K is total profit (if K is paid marginal product) and LF_l Is total wages (if L paid marginal product). This means total output F will equal the sum of competitively determined inputs costs if there are constant returns to scale, $\lambda = 1$. Otherwise, there is a surplus for increasing returns, and a deficit for decreasing returns.

Note that this can all be generalised to n goods, with $y = f(x_1, x_2, ..., x_n)$, returns to scale given by $f(tx_1, tx_2, ..., tx_n) = t^\lambda f(x_1, x_2, ..., x_n)$, and Euler's theorem by $x_1 f_1 + x_2 f_2 + ... x_n f_n = \lambda f$.

So, for Cobb–Douglas, growth of output will appear to be the sum of growth of inputs weighted by (constant) factor shares. By making all of the assumptions for Cobb–Douglas, α can be estimated by finding what value best fits the tracking of growth by weighted factor shares.

Put this on one side for the moment. For any economy, because of national income accounting:

$$Y = rK + wL \tag{5.2}$$

For small changes in these:

$$dY = rdK + wdL + Kdr + Ldw.$$

Divide by Y and fiddle a bit to give:

$$dY/Y = (rK/Y)dK/K + (wL/Y)dL/L + (Kdr/Y + Ldw/Y) \tag{5.3}$$

Suppose factor shares are, indeed, constant so that $rK/Y = \alpha$ and $wL/Y = 1 - \alpha$, and that wage and profit rates are fixed so that the last term in brackets on the right-hand side of (5.3) is zero, then (5.2) becomes the same as (5.2). What this means is that no matter how factor shares are determined (by a fixed monopoly mark-up with lots of excess capacity, for example, as opposed to perfect competition, etc.), because of the national income identity (5.2), it will appear as if the use of Cobb–Douglas is justified. Indeed, the fit in these circumstances should be perfect. It might not be because of numerical errors, approximating discrete by marginal shifts, and change in wages and profit rates rather than these remaining constant (possibly detrended for a productivity change or shift in A, see below). Perversely, though, the failure for the Cobb–Douglas to fit exactly, as it should, gives the impression that there are some errors in some legitimate estimation. Inaccuracy gives the authenticity of legitimacy, leading Anwar Shaikh to deconstruct the whole exercise as humbug (showing a production function would fit data artificially constructed to spell out the word).

In short, constant factor shares are not evidence at all for the presence or legitimacy of a Cobb–Douglas production function. It would simply be an artefact of constant factor shares and national income accounting. The same applies for production functions more generally, and not just for Cobb–Douglas. For $Y = AF(K, L)$: $dY = AF_K dK + AF_L dL$, which after dividing through by Y, etc., becomes:

$$dY/Y = (AKF_K/Y)dK/K + (ALF_L/Y)dL/L \tag{5.4}$$

Once again this mirrors equation (5.3) derived from national income accounts, although in this case, unlike the Cobb–Douglas, there is no need for factor shares to be constant. By allowing the production function to have more parameters (two for example as with the constant elasticity of substitution, see Box 5.2), then it is possible to track shifts in national income more accurately than for the Cobb–Douglas. But this is not evidence for the legitimacy or otherwise of the use of production functions. Or, to put this another way, however well a production function tracks national income, this does not offer support for using a production function nor explain either output growth or distribution since the use of the production function is merely tracking, however well, a national income identity. The latter inevitably incorporates a strong relationship between the growth of output and the growth of inputs weighted by factor shares.

Box 5.2
The constant elasticity of substitution function

As has been seen, the Cobb–Douglas functional form is highly restrictive, not least given the constant and particular values of its corresponding elasticities. A slightly more general functional form is given by the constant elasticity of substitution function. For utility, it would be $u(x_1, x_2) = (\alpha x_1^\rho + \beta x_2^\rho)^{1/\rho}$ where $-\infty < \rho \leq 1$, for parameters, α, β and ρ, with one extra parameter ρ over the Cobb–Douglas. For this functional form, it turns out that the elasticity of substitution, σ, is constant and equals $1/(1 - \rho)$. Recall that $\sigma = 1$, for the Cobb–Douglas utility function, and this corresponds to ρ tending to one in the functional form. For perfect substitutability $\rho = 1$, $u = \alpha x_1 + \beta x_2$ and $\sigma = \infty$; and, for $\rho = -\infty$, $\sigma = 0$ with perfect complements or no substitutability at all.

Despite these results that were known almost as soon as the Cobb–Douglas itself, and that have been unsuccessfully signalled again and again subsequently by heterodox critics of the mainstream, the use of Cobb–Douglas or other production functions seems to have been legitimised by the exercise of tracking national income. Indeed, there is a history of spirited, if illegitimate defence of production functions, primarily on no firmer grounds than this is what we do so let's see how we can justify it (which they cannot even on their own terms).

5.3 Total Factor Productivity

The result of disregarding the lack of legitimacy underpinning production functions has been the commonplace use of the one-sector production function to represent some sort of whole economy. In particular, $Y = AF(K, L)$ with constant returns to scale and diminishing returns to factors. As a result, $Y/L = (1/L)F(K, L) = F(K/L, 1)$ for constant returns. This means that the economy/

production can be represented by a per capita production function, using lower-case notation for per capita variables, $Y/L = y = F(K/L, 1) = f(k)$ – the 1 as second argument can be dropped as it is constant. This can be scaled up for number of workers. For perfect competition, with $Y = Lf(K/L)$ marginal products will equal factor prices, so:

$$r = dY/dK = f'(k),$$

and, slightly more complicated, $w = dY/dL = f - (KL/L^2)f'(k)$ or $w = f(k) - kf'(k)$. With positive but diminishing marginal products, i.e. $f'(k) < 0$, it follows that the relationships between k and y, r and w, are as depicted in Diagram 5.1. Because $r = f'(k)$, it is the diminishing slope to the per capita production function, $y = f'(k)$.

This is nothing other than neoclassical intuition from a one-sector, partial equilibrium model. Output increases with capital intensity, profit rates fall with more capital per worker, but wages rise as labour becomes relatively scarcer. However, such intuitions are already known to be invalid from the TA[2] itself as

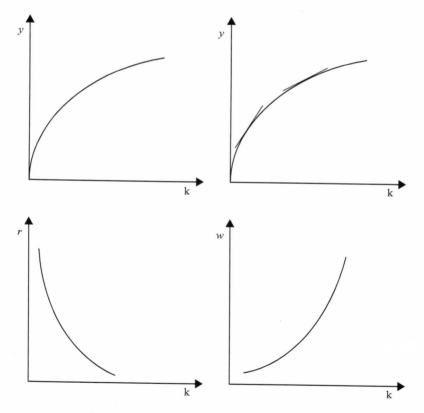

Diagram 5.1   Production functions: false intuitions?

a result of the way in which an economy with many sectors does not behave as if there were one. Indeed, it is anomalous for the mainstream to treat the economy as if it only has one sector in which production and distribution (wage and profit rates from marginal products) are the consequence of supply conditions alone without reference to demand. Utility functions and consumption are notable for their absence from the determinants of production and distribution in the immediately preceding equations.

Despite these issues, from the mid-1950s, starting with classic work by Robert Solow, it became standard to represent an economy by a single production function and, in particular, to use it to *measure* technical change (the emphasis will be explained later). Suppose once more that $Y = AF(K, L)$ and the presumption is that growth in output, Y, comes from a combination of growth in inputs, K and L, and changes in A over time thought to be due to technical progress or productivity increase (if A increases, you get more output from given inputs). Then: $dY = AF_K dK + AF_L dL + FdA$, which, after dividing through by Y, etc., becomes:

$$dY/Y = (AKF_K/Y)dK/K + (ALF_L/Y)dL/L + dA/A.$$

This is just the previous equation (5.4) with dA/A added to allow for A to shift as well as inputs in causing Y to shift. With full employment and perfect competition, as before, AKF_K/Y is the share of capital and ALF_L/Y is the share of labour. Denote these by, not necessarily constant, α and $1 - \alpha$, respectively, and use g<x> to denote the rate of growth of any variable x. Then:

$$g<A> = g<Y> - \alpha g<K> - (1 - \alpha)g<L> \qquad (5.5)$$

g<A> is called total factor productivity (TFP), and is presumed to measure the extent to which there has been a shift in the production function as opposed to a shift along it (see Diagram 5.2). The point of the exercise in what is termed growth accounting is to seek to measure the extent to which a shift from O to N in the figure is due to changes in inputs as opposed to those of the production function itself. So, for example, if inputs each increased by 2 per cent and output by 5 per cent, it might reasonably be inferred that productivity has gone up by 3 per cent. But, if one input, K say, goes up by 1 per cent and the other, L, by 3 per cent, and output again by 5 per cent, productivity seems to have gone up by somewhere between 4 per cent (capital productivity) and 2 per cent (labour productivity). To get a single measure, it is necessary to compile a composite (increase in) input measure by weighting how much each contributes to output. As can be seen from (5.5), to reduce the growth of inputs to a single input index, each input can be weighted by its factor share (which in marginal productivity theory equates to its contribution to output). Put another way, with growth in capital of g<K>, output is expected to rise by αg<K> and, similarly, (1 – α)g<L> for labour. Deduct the sum of these input-induced and input-imputed contributions to output from the actual increase in output and what is left is TFP.

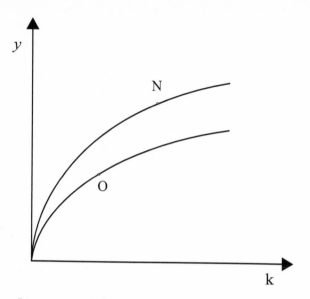

Diagram 5.2   Shift of or along the production function?

As already observed a number of times and should by now be apparent, TFP is merely *measured* by this procedure. As acknowledged by its practitioners, it is a *residual*. Measure the output growth that would be expected from the input changes alone. Any difference from this (it is usually more, for productivity increase over time) is accounted for by TFP interpreted as technical change.

Yet, as is obvious as a residual even on its own terms, what TFP measures is not only shifts in the production function as indicated by shifts in A, but also *all* deviations from the assumptions on which TFP is constructed. In other words, TFP measures deviations (or changes) in conditions of competitiveness and full employment. And it also measures deviations from the assumption that there is a single sector in the economy. In general, this means that K is measured by taking its value in price terms, deflated accordingly. Even if, just for the sake of argument, there was only one consumption good, with price p, and K_1, K_2, ..., K_n, capital goods with prices p_1, p_2, ..., p_n, then the value of capital would be measured by $p_1K_1/p + p_2K_2/p + ... + p_nK_n/p$. Even if relative prices of capital goods, p_1, remain the same, if p changes (say increases for whatever reason on the demand side), then the value of capital would change (fall). This would not be because there had been any change in technology but simply because the value of capital had changed. And, treating the economy as if it had only one good means any change in the *price* of capital must be treated as if it were a change in the *quantity* of capital. Even for an economy with one capital good and one consumption good, with relative price p of the capital in terms of the consumption good, and physical measure of capital m, the value of capital is pm. If this economy is treated as if it only has one sector, then any change in k = pm must be treated as if a change in m. If p increases, this appears as an increase in k even though output has remained the same. So, with apparently more capital and the same level of output (per worker), the conclusion must be drawn of decline in productivity, even though it is demand and not supply (and productivity) that has changed.

This, and some other results as well, can be illustrated more formally in the simplest possible way by considering an economy with just one consumption good and one capital good. This makes the presentation easier than having many more capital and/or consumption goods without affecting the results. Suppose, then, that production comprises two *processes*, one to produce the capital good and one to produce the consumption good. Let a of capital goods and l of labour be used in the production of capital goods, and b and n, similarly and respectively, for the consumption good. Also assume constant returns to scale. The two processes together will be called a *technique*, and a technique corresponds to a single point on the per capita production function, f(k) for a particular value of k. But a technique in this case allows for the production of the consumption good but via, and different from, the capital good, unlike the one-sector production function, f (see Section 5.2 in terms of Lego, etc.). If p is the price of the capital good relative to the consumption good, r is the rate of profit or cost of capital, and is the wage rate for perfect competition:

$$pa(1 + r) + wl = p, \text{ and}$$
$$pb(1 + r) + wn = 1,$$

since the price of the consumption good can be taken to be one or as the numeraire. These equations follow from assuming capital goods are paid for in advance and must be repaid together with the rate of profit/interest, but wages are paid in arrears and so do not attract profit as an advance. If wages were paid in advance as well, it would make no substantive difference to the results, although the algebra is marginally more complicated and the algebraic results slightly different.

Between these two equations, p can be eliminated – the clumsy details are left as an exercise – to give:

$$1 + r = (1 - wn)/(a + wlb - wna).$$

Again, sparing the mathematical details, by differentiating r for w it can be show that this is downward sloping, so that r and w are inversely related. It can also be shown that the curve representing the inverse relationship between w and r is either concave or convex to the origin or a straight line, as lb > na; lb < na; or lb = na; or, equivalently, on the relative magnitudes of a/l and b/n (see Diagram 5.3). Note that these are the physical capital to labour ratios of the two production processes. The graphs are called factor-price frontiers (fpf), and show the relationships between w and r for the given technique. Note, though, that the graphs have been drawn with the w-r axes swapped over from the above equation.

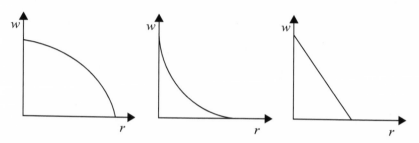

Diagram 5.3　Technique factor price frontiers

As observed, if a/l = b/n, then the technique fpf is linear, and this is equivalent to a situation in which there is in effect only one good in the economy in all but name. For, from the point of view of production, the capital and consumption goods do not differ in composition of inputs with which they are produced; they only differ in the scale of the same ratio of inputs used. If the measurement of the outputs were rescaled, for example, each output would require exactly the same level of inputs. Accordingly, whatever the values of w and r, the prices of the consumption and capital goods will always be in the same ratio as their fixed ratio of use of inputs. If the capital good, for example, uses three times as much of both inputs as the consumption good, then its price will be three times greater wherever the values of w and r settle. Essentially, this is to restore the one-sector world in which the two nominally separate goods are effectively the same since inputs are always usable in the same proportions to produce one or the other (and we do not allow mistakes in producing what is wanted).

By the same token, when a/l ≠ b/n, then the relative prices of the two goods *will* change depending on what the wage and profit rates are, with the more machine-intensive production going up in price as r increases (and w decreases as it must as w and r are inversely related). This is hardly surprising as the more machine-intensive (labour-intensive) good in production becomes relatively more expensive (cheaper) as r increases (w decreases). It might be worth noting in passing that if there are more than two capital goods, such a simple categorisation of the more or less capital-intensive becomes impossible in general as production may be more capital-intensive in one but not another input.

Now, the technique fpf shows the possible combinations of w and r if that technique is in use. It cannot reveal what w and r will be as the economy could settle anywhere on the fpf. But, by analogy with the one-sector production function, there are a whole series of techniques available, each one corresponding to a particular point on the one-sector production function, f. For each technique, there will be a corresponding fpf. Just two are shown in Diagram 5.4. At wage rates above w* (profit rates below r*), technique 1 will be in use since this competitively allows for a higher profit rate (higher wage) than for technique 2, and vice versa for the use of technique 2 with wage below w* (and r above r*). The point (r*, w*) is called a switch point since it represents the values around which one technique rather than the other will be adopted by profit-maximising producers.

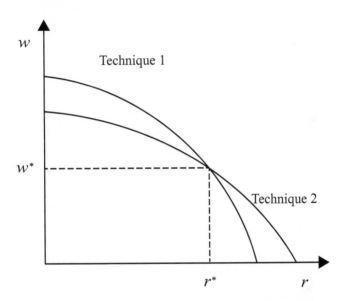

Diagram 5.4   Economy factor price frontier and switch point

So far just two technique fpfs have been put together. To build a full counterpart to the one-sector production function, f, it is necessary to have an infinite set of techniques, with each one corresponding to f for a particular value of k. For f, this is simply a matter of a greater value of k as we substitute capital for labour in the production process and get a higher but diminishing marginal product of capital. For an infinite number of technique fpfs, the economy fpf is traced out as in Diagram 5.5. This is formed from the outside of all of the individual technique fps. A point on the economy fpf must be touched by one or other technique fpf but must also lie outside all the others as well – otherwise the economy fpf would be further out. Any technique fpf that lay totally inside the others would not contribute to the economy fpf. Some other technique would always be able to pay a higher w for a given r or vice versa. Mathematically, the economy fpf is neatly called the 'envelope' of the individual technique fpfs.

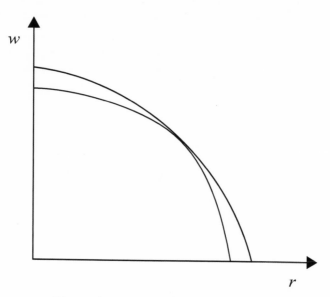

Diagram 5.5   Economy factor price frontier

Now suppose the particular technique in use is known, corresponding to being given k for the one-sector production function from which we can derive both output, $f(k)$, and distribution by taking marginal products so that $r = f'(k)$, the slope of f at k, and $w = f(k) - kf'(k)$. Does the same apply for knowing the technique in use and all techniques available, in parallel with the one-sector model where there is more than one sector? The answer would appear to be yes. This is because the technique fpf can be traced around until it just touches the economy fpf, and that gives r and w (see Diagram 5.5).

In passing, it will also be possible to work out y as well, as long as the distribution of output is known between the consumption and capital goods (which depends on how much there is saving for investment). Given this, to evaluate net output, it is necessary to work out p beforehand. This is possible from either of the equations for the processes, since w and r are both known. Then we can add up the net output of whatever division is produced between consumption and capital goods using the derived p. Note, this means that the value of net output will change if either its composition changes or price changes, with the latter unable to be captured within the one-sector model as there is no relative price between capital and consumption goods. This is at the heart of the problem with the one-sector model and will be finessed as simply as possible in Section 5.4 (by assuming all net output is for consumption) to highlight the fallacies in using the model for empirical work.

However, even for theoretical work things are not so simple, since it is possible that the same technique fpf may touch, or form, the economy fpf at more than one point. For ease of illustration, this will be shown with a downward sloping technique fpf but one that is more wobbly than usual (which would occur if there were more than one capital good, each extra capital good potentially adding an extra downward sloping wobble). In Diagram 5.6 one of the techniques illustrated touches the economy fpf at more than one point. As a result, it is impossible to derive distribution from knowledge of technology as a whole and which technique is in use (and the same applies to output, as p will be different between the two points and y evaluated differently accordingly). The same technique could be the one in use at both high and low levels of profitability (wages). This goes entirely against the logic of the intuition of the mainstream one-sector production function for which k is used just once in association with a definite level of output and distribution between r and w.

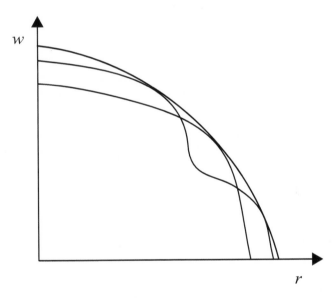

Diagram 5.6   Reswitching

Given the technique is profitable at two separate profit rates, there must be some other techniques that are most profitable in between. One of these is illustrated in Diagram 5.6. It is relatively easy to see that this technique must cut across the original at least twice since the original goes above it to the envelope on two occasions. So the two techniques have more than one switching point with one another. This is called double or, more generally, reswitching (of techniques). So, a necessary condition for not being able to derive distribution from knowledge of all techniques (equivalent to f) and the one in use (k) is that there should be no reswitching.

As a result, some mainstream economists have argued, and most have assumed, that whether the one-sector production function remains valid or not is an empirical question, contingent upon whether reswitching exists in the real world, although this has rarely if ever been investigated in practice in this context. It is a sweet irony that the mainstream turns to realism, and the empirical evidence, when its own technical apparatus, principles and practices come under threat, whilst such realism is blissfully ignored in establishing those principles. In any case, reswitching is common in practice with, for example, nuclear power (with high capital costs both in the present and the long distant future, i.e. waste disposal) tending to be more profitable at both high and low rates of interest.

But the deeper theoretical point is that the one-sector production function is invalid as a representation of an economy (or, more accurately, a model of an economy) with more than one good, not least one in which demand considerations can be left aside on the mainstream's own terms of how to view the economy. The one-sector model is simply that, and not a simplified version of a more complex model as far as its theoretical results are concerned (distribution and output determined by f and k, for example). This is little more than saying what the mainstream has known all along: that partial equilibrium is not a good representation of general equilibrium (see Chapter 3). Even if it is possible, in the absence of reswitching, to work out distribution from knowledge of production alone, this does little to explain why that particular technique is in use. It could be that the wage was fixed externally, by the state or trade unions for example, leading that technique to be adopted. Either way, it does not follow that the marginal product of capital (which cannot be defined, as marginal changes along the economy fpf lead to changes in both quantity of capital and its price) can be used to determine what the profit rate is. Indeed, the determination runs in the opposite direction, needing to know r before knowing k or the technique in use.

5.4 Measuring Something Called TFP in Practice

Despite these issues, and the attempts of heterodox economists over the past 50 years to highlight them, the one-sector production function continues to be used for both theoretical *and* empirical purposes. For the latter, the deficiencies in its use for measuring TFP do not depend at all upon the presence or otherwise of reswitching (although this is often confused in mainstream accounts, as if the theoretical requirement carried over to the empirical work).

Consider the following per capita national income identity, $y = kr + w$. From this it follows that: $k = (y - w)/r$. Assume, if only for simplicity of graphical exposition, that there is no growth in the economy, so that net output is entirely in terms of the consumption good. Then y will be the same as the maximum wage since all net per capita output would be going to wages. As a result, if the economy were on the technique fpf at A for a particular technique, then k = (y − w)/r is given by the tangent of angle CAB, as in Diagram 5.7. Now consider a different technique altogether, presumed to touch the economy fpf at A' (Diagram 5.8). This has been cleverly constructed so that the angle at A' is exactly the same as at A. As a result, the value of capital, k, at the two points will be the same. But the level of output, y, is very different having declined between the two. The reason is that the fall in amount of the capital stock is equal and opposite to the increase in its value, p. As it were k = pm = p'm', with p and m moving in equal and opposite directions between A and A'.

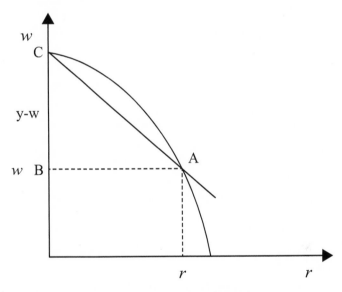

Diagram 5.7   Value of capital

As a result, even though there has been no change in technology or techniques available to the economy, merely a shift from one technique to another, there will be measured a decline in TFP. This is because y has gone down, from C to C' − recall that the intercept on the y-axis is maximum wage and net output − but measured k has remained the same. In other words, less y for the same k: a decline in TFP.

More generally than for this example, as observed, TFP measures technical change as a residual and incorporates any deviation from its assumptions as well as any technical change itself, with the two simply being conflated with one another. The assumptions include treating the economy as if it can be represented by a single good. This means treating any change in the price system

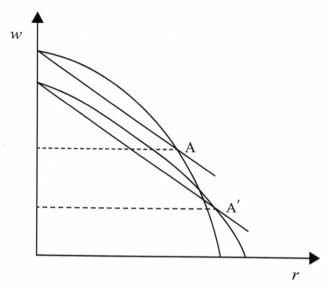

Diagram 5.8   Value of capital constant as output changes with no technical change

(derived from shifts in demand even for the mainstream), reflected in changes in the value of capital, k, as if it were necessarily a change in the quantity of capital, as if a change in p were a change in m. Accordingly, even the modest task of measuring TFP as a residual is fundamentally flawed and to a large degree incoherent, as if trying to measure the area of a rectangle when only given the dimensions of one side (let alone dealing in the higher dimensions of more than one capital good).

5.5 From Mismeasurement to Misinterpretation

In Chapter 4, the example was given of Adam Smith's preoccupation with the productivity that derives from the growing division of labour within a factory, and how this was taken further by Karl Marx in his own theory of how accumulation of capital is attached to a contingent interaction between economies of scale and scope. Further, Marx is universally recognised amongst scholars for his close attention to how production is organised and evolves to and through the factory system, in which workers are commanded to work up ever more raw materials into final products in the drive for higher productivity and profit.

Further, Joseph Schumpeter is famous for the notion of creative destruction in which a particular interdependent technological system needs to be destroyed, not least by recession, before it can be displaced by another (as with transition from steam to electricity as a major source of power), leading to long waves of economic activity as the consequence of the rise and decline of technologies, and corresponding levels of investments and economic activity. This has been further developed into the idea that there are particular national systems of innovation that are more or less conducive to technological change depending on relations across education and skills, research and development, corporate strategies and state policies.

What each of these different approaches share in common is, explicit or otherwise, a critical point of departure from production narrowly conceived as the simple physical transformation of inputs into outputs. By contrast, production takes place alongside definite workplace relations and in a definite external environment that is more or less conducive to productivity increase (which itself needs to be carefully construed, distinguishing across working for longer, more intensively, more productively, in different ways and forms of organisation, and different production processes and products). In this light, especially if also attaching production to power relations and those of hierarchy, with different meanings and motives to workers and bosses alike, the production function is rendered dead as a dodo. But long live the production function, since it can always seek to reduce these other considerations to being one or more input or one or more output. Such is a strategy for economics imperialism, and it has been highly successful in capturing the separate and independent disciplines of industrial relations and industrial sociology, and turning them into human resource management.

And, for a theory of technical change, as opposed to the flawed measurement of TFP, there is always the option of imposing TA^2. This has been most obvious in treating technical change, or innovation, either as something that is produced – you guessed it – by a production function according to resources put in as inputs with productivity increase as output, as with expenditure on research and development with output measured by patents for example. Or technical change can be perceived as an externality deriving from learning on the job, for example, or from spillover from another firm.

In short, the limited ambitions and achievements of the mainstream theory of production and technological change are a direct consequence of its core reliance upon TA^2. This is apparent in seeking to measure and understand technical change in terms of production functions as well, if often more in the background, perceiving the architecture of the economic system as a whole in terms of the aggregated behaviour of optimising individuals.

5.6 Further Thoughts and Readings

One of the most striking aspects of the application of the TFP framework is what happens after the residual has been calculated, for then the evolving pattern of changing productivity is bereft of explanation. Why did this economy, sector, etc. perform well with high growth apparently due to high TFP, or why did this one perform so badly? Remarkably, the most common answer is to appeal to explanatory factors that have already been precluded by the assumptions necessary to calculate TFP in the first place. For example, TFP was low because of a recession (you might have thought anyone would know that anyway, but it means perfectly competitive markets are violated – invalidating the TFP calculations that you are trying to explain) or because of the rise of trade unions demanding too high wages or obstructing introduction of new techniques (what happened to the perfect labour markets on which TFP was calculated). For criticism of case studies of this sort, see Fine (1992) on the South African apartheid coal industry (hardly subject to perfect competition) and Sato (2005) on the South Korean steel industry (with the largest plants in the world, hardly subject to constant returns to scale).

For a simple exposition of the critique of the one-sector production function (the Cambridge Capital Critique or Controversies) along the lines presented here, and for its broader implications, see Fine (1980). For the spurious reliance upon Cobb–Douglas and more, see Felipe and McCombie (2013). For accounts of the studious neglect of these issues, see Hodgson (1997) and Cohen and Harcourt (2003). And for some background history, see Carter (2011, 2011/12, 2012).

6
Labour Markets

6.1 Overview

This chapter begins by posing the issue of whether labour markets are like any other. This question raises difficult problems for the mainstream since, in view of its universal principles around the technical apparatus and technical architecture of microeconomics (TA²), it would treat labour like any other contribution to production and (dis)utility. On the other hand, the labour market is unavoidably different from other markets (although the same might be said of other markets too, not least land and finance, if in different ways). Not surprisingly, as covered in Section 6.3, the mainstream starting point for labour market analysis does take it to be like others and, on this basis, has been organised around human capital theory. This is subject to critical assessment for the way in which it treats skills (as if produced by resources or market imperfections) and for the way in which it sees them as being rewarded (according to their productivity, however accurately given market imperfections). Not surprisingly, human capital theory is riddled with tensions around such a starting point and acknowledging the varieties of ways in which the labour market is not constituted in this way in light of the underlying factors that condition both the demand and the supply sides.

As addressed in Section 6.4, such conundrums have been incorporated into the mainstream by suggesting at most that labour markets work imperfectly, especially because of informational asymmetries with, for example, the model of efficiency wages to the fore. This allows for certain anomalies within labour markets to be explained, not least the existence of labour market structures (between the employed and unemployed, occupational segregation and apparently unjustified wage differentials, for example). But, paradoxically, such richness in specifying labour markets is accompanied by a set of theoretical principles (around asymmetric information) that do not distinguish labour markets. In addition, the reduction of the complexity of labour markets to market imperfections has the effect of setting aside issues of class, conflict and power.

Following a digression of the distinction between risk and uncertainty in Section 6.5, in which it is suggested that the exclusive attention to one at the expense of the other yields unexpected benefits in explaining market imperfections, some attention is devoted to the minimum wage debate in Section 6.6.

This has attracted enormous attention because the empirical evidence seemed to challenge the mainstream nostrum that increasing, or establishing, an effective minimum wage does not necessarily reduce employment. The conclusion drawn is not to settle on one or other side of the debate but, rather, to suggest that labour markets simply do not function in a way that is reducible to supply and demand with more or less refinement.

This leads to a discussion in Section 6.7 of segmented, following dual, labour market theory, and the idea that labour markets are structured by both supply- and demand-side factors that are as much social as economic. And it is also concluded that labour markets are not only segmented into different structures but that they are also internally differentiated in how each of these structured labour markets generate corresponding wages and conditions of work.

6.2 From Labour as Fish ...

The mainstream microeconomics of labour markets is dominated by the idea that the labour market is like any other in the sense of being subject to exactly the same principles of analysis as all other markets, which are presumed themselves to be subject analytically to common and universal principles. The focus for employment, as for all else, is upon what determines supply and demand and how they interact with one another. At the crudest level, often projected to span both micro and macro, it follows that if there is any unemployment, then there must be an excess supply of labour and real wages (or some other reward to labour such as employment rights or fringe benefits) that are too high and which should adjust downwards to bring about market equilibrium by reducing supply and increasing demand. Of course, appeal to market imperfections, whether at the micro or macro levels, might be used to justify state intervention (see below on minimum wages and also varieties of Keynesian theory for the macroeconomics of involuntary unemployment).

Does this mean that the market for labour is the same as the market for fish? Some mainstream economists suggest not, since workers are human and can think and behave for themselves unlike fish or, possibly more appropriately, ping pong balls, as the latter do not act on their own account whereas fish at least seek to evade capture. However, both fish and ping pong balls may not be able to bring themselves to the market to trade but they do have, as it were, representatives to trade on their behalf. And much the same is true of trade unions in representing their members in the labour market (does this make them more or less fish-like or manipulated dupes as those who oppose trade unionism would have it?). Even those who are not unionised, and are taken on in the labour market casually and individually, are in a sense represented by the norms governing the exercise of labour however much these are or are not observed in practice. Significantly, the social theorist, Karl Polanyi, argued that land, labour and finance were three commodities for which treating them like any other would ultimately lead to a social reaction against such commodification and in favour of reasserted forms of social control, what he called a 'double movement' between treating them as if they were ordinary commodities and in opposition to doing so. It is not clear, though, that such a double movement is confined to these three commodity markets alone, since all commodities and markets are governed by shifting regulations and norms to a greater or lesser extent. Nor is there any reason why those buying and selling commodities of any sort should not be equally subject to motives other than self-interest, or be governed by independent thought and social norms, and so going beyond targeting the bottom line in the accounts or in pursuit of self-interest.

In short, what distinguishes labour markets is not the agency of those doing the selling (the employee) or the buying (the employer), but the nature of what is bought and sold. Karl Marx offers the most sophisticated analysis of this issue, highlighting that there is not and cannot be a 'labour' market, for it is not labour as such that is bought and sold (as, for example, an input into a production function) but the *capacity* to work. For Marx, only under capitalism is the capacity to work bought and sold with the wage as its price. Under other economic systems, such as slavery, the capacity to work is not bought and sold other than indirectly through the purchase of the labourers themselves.

These considerations point to a conclusion that has already been advanced in the context of other microeconomic topics – for consumption, production, competition and technical change – that the microeconomic needs to be set in its historical and social context. This is exactly the opposite of the way in which the mainstream proceeds. On the basis of its technical apparatus, labour markets are conceptually embedded in universal categories, only after which their social and historical specificity is addressed. To put it polemically, is slave labour and wage labour the same as labour, merely being allocated to production in different ways?

For the mainstream, the answer would appear to be yes, at least insofar as labour is simply treated as an input into a production function like any other input and like any production, $Y = F(K, L)$. Likewise, labour can be introduced as a variable in the utility function, although this is considered negatively as contributing to disutility (and, once again, it might be asked if the disutility of slave and wage labour are the same if the same work is done for the same amount of time without regard to the context in which the work is done).

Interestingly, the disutility of labour has taken two very different forms in the mainstream. The first has been met before in Chapter 3 (see Diagram 3.2). It reflects the idea that labour is a resource of time that the worker has but is able to give up and sell to the employer. What is given up, or foregone, is the positive contribution made to utility by leisure. What is done with that leisure time is rarely examined although, no doubt, it is considerably enhanced in quality by the goods that can be purchased in return for the wages earned by the leisure given up.

The second way of looking at work, most prominently at the time of the marginalist revolution of the 1870s but subsequently less to the fore, is that work itself is a disutility and not just the resource of time foregone in sacrificing leisure. Significantly, to see labour markets in terms of the *disutility* of work is potentially to raise the issue of why this should be so. It could be the work itself, although it might be thought that hard labour is no more wearisome than the leisure centre exercise that has become so popular amongst some. Indeed, that work itself is a disutility is not a universal experience, for the most arduous and demanding work, mental and physical, can be rewarding and be undertaken without remuneration whether for the pleasure/utility of the activity itself, or for other motives than to secure financial reward (as in much domestic labour, especially that of upbringing and caring especially if more equitably shared). For the antipathy to work derives as much from how it is done, for whom, under whose command and for what purpose as for the nature of the work itself, although this clearly varies over the type of labour involved and individual capabilities and motivations. This reinforces the point that the putative (dis) utility of work is different in weight and meaning under capitalism compared to other economic systems, and even within capitalism whether depending on waged labour, and what sort, or otherwise.

Although there is a difference between receiving a wage for giving up (leisure) time and suffering disutility from the work itself, there is no reason why both of these should not be considered together and, in production or utility functions, each appears as a quantum of labour if negatively in the utility function. Over time, though, the sacrifice of leisure has taken precedence over the disutility aspect. But the latter has not been discarded altogether. In brief for the moment, this is because (as in the simple general equilibrium model of Chapter 3) the understanding of labour as a resource allows a Pareto efficient outcome to be identified (for Robinson Crusoe). Subsequently, though, the idea of labour as a disutility can be brought back into the analysis to explain why achievement of the Pareto efficient outcome might be thwarted by, for example, the work-shy, disutility-avoiding action of workers if they are able to get away with supposedly selling their labour but not delivering it. In other words, what is taken to be the disutility aspect of work serves as a proxy for the social and historical context of wage work itself, as well as the rationale for explaining why labour markets might work inefficiently.

6.3 ... To Human Capital Theory

With labour as a resource that is bought and sold as on any other market, and unemployment explained purely and simply as the consequence of the real wage being too high, human capital theory came to prominence within labour market theory from the 1950s onwards. This has the goal of explaining why some workers are paid more than others in light of the skills that they bring to their work. Given the problem it posed to itself of explaining wage differentials, it is a fortunate convenience for the mainstream that the disutility of work is secondary within labour market theory since, as was observed by Adam Smith at the end of the eighteenth century, the most arduous and undesirable work is often paid the least. Leaving this anomaly aside, human capital theory comprises two elements.

One is to address how skills, or human capital, are created, and the other is to explain how those skills are rewarded. For the creation of human capital, in parallel with the theory of technical change, the mainstream draws upon its technical apparatus in two ways. Either it is the result of the allocation of dedicated resources, possibly incorporated into a production function for skills, or it is the result of a market imperfection such as an externality, the leading example of which is on-the-job learning – or, in other words, you gain skills through the process of work itself, whether by practice or collaboration.

For the deliberate production of human capital, the most popular point of reference is education, with qualifications, years of study and the like as an index of its level, whether for an individual or for an economy. This is to reduce education and the education system as if it were purely designed for vocational purposes. But education plays a much wider role than this, ranging from socialisation through to learning for the sheer pleasure (utility even) it brings as opposed to productivity increase and its rewards. Not surprisingly, the empirical relationship between resources allocated, to schooling say, and educational achievement is far from strong since resources as such, whether educational budgets or pupil study time, are significant but far from the sole determinants of outcomes (and levels of resources alone do not always create good or bad schools or education systems).

This is indicative of the way in which human capital theory tends to be blind to the social and historical factors that underpin the educational process. This is because education is reduced to inputs in and outputs out without regard to the wider roles that education plays in reflecting and creating social norms in which, for example, gender roles are particularly prominent – as much in vocational as other education and learning. Nor is it surprising that educational curricula should be controversial precisely because vocational goals and roles are both contested and not necessarily predominant.

Consideration of other sources of skills, such as work experience, represents a token, if welcome, acknowledgement that production involves work itself and not simply the purchase of inputs in the most efficient proportions. Once again, though, such skills should not be reduced to a technical relationship alone. For, especially within the workplace, what and who counts as skilled are also highly contested, not least along gender lines, and it is further mixed in with who is a good worker in the sense of displaying hard work and loyalty.

There are good reasons, then, for doubting human capital theory for the ways in which it understands what skills are and how they are created. But human capital theory has been less conceptually and theoretically driven in these respects and more attuned to its second goal or element, not merely explaining the nature and origins of skills but how they lead to wage differentials. Such empirical work takes as its starting point an equation to be estimated of the following sort, with obvious notion where the X_i are various conditioning variables, see below:

$$w = a + bHC + c_1X_1 + c_2X_1 + c_3X_2 + ...$$

On this basis, not only can the wage premium, b, be found for a level of human capital, however measured, but also the (private) returns to education for the individual if the costs of that education are calculated. If so much by way of resources is laid out on acquiring human capital over the years, so much extra is earned in return – being much like an investment project, the return on the investment can be calculated like that on any other. In addition, by running similar regressions for the whole economy using growth, say, as the dependent variable instead of w, social as opposed to private returns can also be calculated as the benefits that accrue to society as a whole, as opposed to the returns to individuals, from increasing human capital in the economy as a whole. These social returns tend to exceed private returns, and private returns tend to exceed those from other investments. The palatable conclusion to be drawn by those within mainstream economics of education is that there must be market imperfections in and around the provision of human capital with too little being invested by individuals and society as a result of market imperfections (positive externalities in the generation and use of education do not accrue through the market, and finance may not be made available to fund educational investments since these cannot be detached from the individual in case of failure to repay loans). These imperfections should be addressed by policy, either by allowing for a fuller scope of the market (education vouchers for example) at one extreme or by state provision at the other (because of market imperfections in provision of education and/or how it is financed).

There are, however, a number of serious problems with this account. First, and most general, is that the theory of human capital is a disguised application of the one-sector production function approach to both the provision of education and how it is rewarded. Second, as a result, calculations of the returns to education are nothing of the sort. Rather, they do represent this but only much too deeply buried alongside all of the deviations from the assumptions that are necessary for the theory – that there is only one good (even though an education alongside other sectors), that there is perfect competition in all markets, including those for labour, and that there is full employment (the return to education of the unemployed is presumably zero). Third, the results from the regression themselves indicate that markets are not perfect and yet returns are calculated as if they were. This can be seen in two ways. On the one hand, as observed the differences in social and private rates of return to education and between them, and returns on other investments, are indicative of market imperfections. On the other hand, the regression itself uses a whole range of conditioning variables indicative of market imperfections. For these include gender, race, presence of trade unions, capital intensity and competitive structure (how much monopolised, and how much open to trade). But these variables suggest that the labour market is not perfectly competitive, as the impact of the conditioning variables should be negligible, which they are not.

It is also, then, a moot point whether the conditioning variables are the tail that wags the dog of wage determination by human capital. Thus, for example, wage discrimination of 20 per cent or more persists between men and women even after correcting for differences in human capital and despite, in the UK, the longstanding presence of equal pay legislation (equal pay for equal work, although hard to pin down empirically and judicially). The reasons for this are to be found in occupational segregation; men and women do tend to be paid equally if doing exactly the same job but men tend to do better paid jobs. It is also appropriate to observe that such gendered wage discrimination is reinforced by a range of other variables around access to the labour market, not least in light of responsibilities for childcare, for example.

It is not farfetched to suggest that the human capital theory regression does not even begin to get to grips with how labour markets function, as is evident from the regression itself. However much it is theoretically motivated by production functions and the like, it has simply become a throw-in-any-variable to wage determination and see what we get (and, if in log terms, it suggests a universally applicable Cobb–Douglas functional form for producing the wage level). There is no need for a theory for this. And how the independent variables mutually condition one another, and which are present and which are not (potentially seriously affecting the results of the regression), is left on one side.

Whilst these issues can be addressed to some degree through more sophisticated theory and estimation, they are indicative of the way in which the mainstream approach has been based upon socially and historically decontextualising labour markets by excluding many determinants, only to bring them back in again as qualifying factors. As it were, the results of human capital theory suggest that women are discriminated against in wages received and in access to skills and jobs. This might be explained by a taste for discrimination on the part of employers (subject to competitive erosion) or how minor biological differences become enormously amplified by life choices around investment in education. It makes sense for women to have lower levels of investment in human capital since they are responsible for childcare and will earn a lower rate of return on such investments than men, reinforcing what are taken to be given relatively minor biological differences in the first instance. This explanation is offered in the context of deviations from markets perceived as working perfectly; minor can become even bigger differences when markets work imperfectly (see Section 6.4) since being a woman is taken as a proxy for being of lower skill even if this is not so for the individual woman as opposed to the average for women.

6.4 Imperfect Labour Markets

Such issues reflect marked tensions within the mainstream in two different ways. One is over treating labour markets as if they are like any other, the other is over whether labour markets work perfectly or imperfectly. The first tension has remained unresolved within the mainstream (as it must if relying upon a universal set of principles, specifically applied to labour markets), whilst the second has increasingly shifted in favour of viewing labour markets as if working imperfectly, especially in microeconomics as opposed to macroeconomics (where, perversely in light of the developments in microeconomics, the unemployment problem is still oriented around elementary micro principles in targeting lower wages to increase employment directly or indirectly through lower inflation and inflationary expectations).

This shift is especially notable in the idea of labour markets as imperfect because of information asymmetries. One particular example of this is the idea of what is known as efficiency wages. This notion has its origins in the context of developing countries in which there are surpluses of labour, raising the question of why wages are not driven down to zero. The answer is that if this were done, workers would be so physically and mentally impaired that their capacity to work, and productivity, would suffer unduly. In other words, productivity is a function of the wage itself. The more you pay, at least beyond some sort of minimum, the more you seem to get effective labour in return. In formal terms, the effective labour supply is $a(w)L$ for some function a and labour force, L, with both w and L chosen by the employer. $a(w)$ might be as illustrated in Diagram 6.1.

Now the employer maximises profits by choosing both what wage to pay and how much labour to employ, with product price, p, and production function, F:

$$\Pi = pF(a(w)L) - wL$$
$$d\Pi/dw = pa'(w)LF'(a(w)L) - L$$
$$d\Pi/dL = pa(w)F'(a(w)L) - w.$$

Setting these two partial differentiations equal to zero, and with much cancelling, it follows that $a'(w) = a(w)/w$. In other words, the wage will be set where the

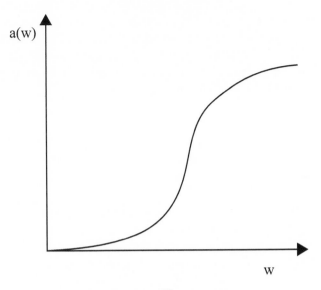

Diagram 6.1   Efficiency wages

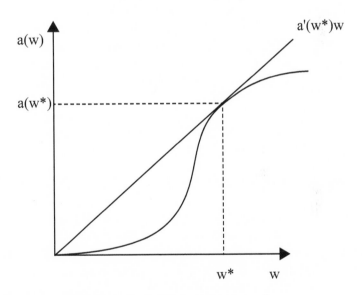

Diagram 6.2   The efficient wage: a'(w) = a(w)/w

marginal efficiency wage equals the average efficiency wage; if not, then it would be possible to get more efficiency labour by increasing the wage – for example, if the marginal were greater than the average as the extra wages would be outweighed by the higher productivity (and vice versa if marginal less than average efficiency wage). This is illustrated in Diagram 6.2 for the equilibrium efficiency wage w*.

There are two remarkable technical results here. First, the wage has been determined independently of the production function (but we normally expect the wage to be set by the marginal product of labour, something like $F'(L)$). This is because the wage is found that maximises the efficiency of labour irrespective of how it is used by reference to the production function. Having found w^*, the production function, F, will merely decide how much labour to employ in light of the output price, p, from one of the equations for profit maximisation. Second, then, the wage, w^*, is set independently of the labour supply. This is not quite correct since the presumption is one of a labour surplus economy, one in which the supply of labour (far) exceeds the demand at the wage, w^*. If there were a shortage of labour at this wage, then labour supply-side factors would come into consideration, as there would not necessarily be sufficient labour supply at the efficiency wage, w^*.

The efficiency wage model also exhibits two further remarkable analytical features. The first is that the real wage does not fall to clear the labour market (set supply and demand equal) even though it is free to do so. Employers choose to hold the wage above the equilibrium level between supply and demand as this is more profitable for them than paying lower wages. Thus, the labour market does not clear despite the absence of institutional barriers to downward wages, unless this is how the physical dependence of labour on a sufficiently high standard of living is to be interpreted. Second, even though the model is based upon the optimising behaviour of individuals, especially employers but also employees who will work at any wage going, a definite labour market structure emerges rather than being assumed. There is a division between the employed and the unemployed even though those on either side of the divide may be otherwise identical to one another.

These results on efficiency wages make no reference to asymmetric information. But this is how more recent mainstream labour market economics has used them in more recent times, shifting from labour surplus to fully developed economies where physical and mental well-being arising out of poverty wages does not appear to be an issue. The argument is that in such economies, the employer at most knows about the average attributes of workers and not their individual attributes in detail, such as skills, motivation and loyalty. So, all employers can do is offer a wage and choose how many to employ across those who show themselves willing to work at that wage. The better workers are presumed to have more favourable alternatives than the worse. As a result, the higher the wage that the employer offers, the better is the average productivity of those who offer themselves for employment. This is exactly the situation on average that prevailed previously, in case productivity depends upon the wage for reasons of physical capacities.

Consider, for example, a situation in which most workers are clustered around an average productivity but some are higher and some are lower. Then, it makes sense for the employer to place the wage slightly higher than the average productivity so that the average productivity of those employed will be dominated by those with average productivity. This is so even if it leads to excess supply of labour at that wage. For, if the wage were dropped below the average productivity, the decline in the average quality of those employed would not be compensated for by the lower levels of wages paid.

In this case, once again then, even though they could be set lower, wages do not fall to clear the labour market because employers choose to hold wages higher as it is more profitable for them to do so in light of the average quality of worker attracted. And a structure is created between the employed and unemployed which does not reflect individual differences (even though they are there) so much as the distribution of differences as a whole and the difference in information that the individual worker has about himself or herself as opposed to what potential employers know about individuals.

To some extent, employers can adopt a more refined strategy in making employment decisions by seeking to close the asymmetric information gap. One way is to use qualifications, references and experience as proxies for worker characteristics. Such methods are known as screening. One problem then is how accurate screening is, not least because, as a second problem, once it is known that screening is being used to pay higher wages and in hiring, workers have an incentive to gain the necessary qualifications even if it is inefficient or deceptive for them to do so as in what is termed credentialism. Screening may lead to the inefficient use of resources to get credentials, either honestly or dishonestly, in pursuit of higher wages and employment chances. In addition, screening may reinforce the labour market structures that are created by other factors. Thus, so it is argued, whilst men and women may on average have different degrees of career breaks for bearing children, and presuming this adversely affects productivity (which is far from proven), then employers may choose to employ and train men over women, even though particular women may not be intending to have children. Note, however, in the simplest model, of efficiency wages, the wage itself is being used as a screening device, sorting between those who will or will not work at that wage and with a corresponding level of productivity.

In short, asymmetric information within labour markets would appear to open up a multiplicity of ways in which labour markets differ from other markets, not least being able to explain the presence of labour market structures (such as occupational structures and wage differentials) as the consequence of the optimising behaviour of both employers and employees. But, as observed in Chapter 1, asymmetric information and its consequences for markets are not unique to labour. Exactly the same principles can apply in other markets, with the most famous and initial example being the market for 'lemons', American slang for poor quality second hand cars. Favoured examples are, for example,

Box 6.1
Moral hazard, adverse selection and beyond

Both moral hazard and adverse selection have entered into the lexicon of mainstream microeconomics as a result of the rising use of asymmetric information as a factor underpinning the microeconomics of market failure. But they are different from one another, with moral hazard primarily arising out of informational asymmetry after the act of exchange (is the exchange delivered upon), and adverse selection arising beforehand (how do we know what is being bought and sold).

In the case of adverse selection, a price is declared for a good of variable quality but, whilst the quality of a particular item may be known to the seller, the level of quality, or other characteristics, is unknown to the buyer. At the declared price, each seller with an item of worth below the offered price will be willing to sell, and the buyer will have to take pot luck with the average quality of the item that comes to market. As the declared price rises, so does the average quality of the good. Looking at this the other way around, this is indicative of adverse selection, in the sense that the better quality sellers choose to stay away from the market until the price reaches their level of quality but, of course, those items of lower quality are far from deterred by a lower price if it remains above their value. This is the basis of the classic market for lemons and for the efficiency wage.

As indicated, moral hazard concerns the quality of what is bought and sold after, not before, the exchange takes place where, for example, it is impossible, difficult or costly for whoever is purchasing to guarantee the quality of what they have purchased. The classic example is insurance, where those who are insured may make false claims of losses or reduce the incentive to protect their property precisely because they do not bear the cost of the loss. One way around this, of course, is to have no claims bonuses or excesses on claims (the first part of a claim must be paid by the insured). Moral hazard is also perceived to apply to labour markets, not least because of the presumed disutility of work and, hence, the failure to deliver work contracted for.

Another instance of market imperfections in the microeconomics of labour markets has been what is called implicit contract theory. In this case, the idea is that there are missing markets for insurance against unemployment (because, for example, of moral hazard – if you are insured against unemployment and loss of wages, no doubt you will give up trying to get a job). So what employers (who may be less risk averse) do, is to guarantee employment and wages in a downturn in return for relatively lower wages in an upturn. This might explain why wages do not rise so much in a boom, and fall so much in a recession, even though this might appear to be necessary to clear the labour market.

financial markets (where borrowers know more about themselves than lenders, so-called adverse selection), damage insurance (where those insured cannot be guaranteed to look after their property or not to make false claims, so-called moral hazard) and health insurance (where the sick know more about themselves than insurers, adverse selection again) (see Box 6.1). In each of these and all other cases, including labour, there are three possibilities: that markets may clear but be Pareto inefficient (some higher productivity workers would be willing to work for a higher wage and some employers would be willing to pay but cannot identify who is high and low productivity for sure, so that the higher productivity workers inefficiently go elsewhere); that markets may not clear (the higher than market-clearing efficiency wage attracts more workers than employers are prepared to take on); and there may be an absence of markets altogether (if, for example, offering higher wages always continues to attract a heavier weight of unskilled as opposed to skilled workers relative to that wage so that there is no optimum efficiency wage, with the higher wage not attracting sufficiently higher productivity). Further, as also mentioned in Chapter 1, asymmetric information allows for non-market factors to be explained in terms of collective responses to market imperfections. Thus, just as second hand car dealers might set up a warranty system to justify higher prices for their higher quality cars, so professional associations, trade unions even, could be explained as a way of reducing informational asymmetries around the quality and commitment of workers.

6.5 Risk and Uncertainty

Asymmetric information does not distinguish labour markets as such, although it does make provision for a wider range of previously excluded factors to be incorporated into the analysis, not least how you might induce workers to overcome presumed work shyness, and reduce monitoring costs, by paying workers a little more than you have to so that they self-discipline for fear of getting the sack should they slack. However, given that asymmetric information does so much within mainstream economics in understanding how markets work imperfectly, it is worth focusing on how information is understood at all, let alone that it should be asymmetric or imperfect (across individuals).

Here there are two important starting points. The first is the longstanding distinction between risk and uncertainty, first highlighted in the 1930s within economics, although the two are often confused with one another terminologically. Formally, risk is essentially the same as probability, referring to a situation in which a number of *known* outcomes are possible, and probabilities, however accurate and however obtained, can be assigned to those outcomes by optimising individuals. In other words, there is a given set of prospective states of the world, x_i, for example (where the x might be vectors of goods to fit in a utility function although possibly just income), with corresponding probabilities p_i. Consequently, individuals can have preferences not only over outcomes but also over mixtures of outcomes of these states with different levels of probabilities attached to them. Typically, then, there could be preferences over bundles of income with different chances of having them – a bit like gambling without the fun of the game. Most simply, for example, do I prefer £100 with certainty or

£200 on the toss of a coin? Or how much on a toss of a coin would I consider to be equivalent to £100 with certainty?

Although the word certainty was just used to indicate 100 per cent probability in a comparison with risky alternatives, the term uncertainty refers to a situation in which the outcomes are *unknowable* or to which probabilities cannot be reasonably assigned (as in an egg balanced on its tip and the different probabilities of the directions in which it might fall). It is inescapable that the world is uncertain since otherwise we would know all possible futures in advance and there could be neither innovation nor discovery. Inevitably, uncertainty creates huge difficulties for the mainstream as it cannot fit into TA^2. For this reason, it is a major factor in the criticism of the mainstream, however much valid, by both post-Keynesian macroeconomists (who see uncertainty as underpinning the volatile role played by money and financial markets for example) and neoliberal (neo-)Austrians who argue that uncertain change is best promoted and coordinated through the market to allow individuals both to innovate and to respond to innovation (as opposed to optimising in purely known or knowable, if potentially probabilistic, conditions).

As a result of lack of comfort with uncertainty, the second starting point for the mainstream is that consideration of it should be simply discarded, leading more generally to knowledge (of the economy) being reduced to information (without the need for interpretation of the contested meanings of that information) and information, in particular, being reduced to knowable quantities, such as price levels, with assigned probabilities – that is, to quantifiable risk alone. This is a questionable procedure. Consider, for example, the risk/uncertainty of Greece abandoning the euro or the UK voting to leave the EU. What these are and what these mean can hardly be reduced to quantifiable risky – that is, probabilistic – alternatives.

This slippage within the mainstream from uncertainty to risk, or excision of uncertainty, is marked by the fate of how 'expectations' have been treated within economics. Keynes brought it to the fore and understood expectations very much in terms of the uncertainty generated within the economic and social system as a whole, and especially around waves of optimism or pessimism (so-called animal spirits). With the resurgence of monetarism with Milton Friedman in the 1970s, and the vertical Phillips curve, expectations became associated with the individual forming estimates of the future price level, and in a sophisticated fashion with the subsequent emergence of rational expectations.

Such developments reflect an increasing affinity between mainstream microeconomics and macroeconomics in the treatment of risk and the corresponding neglect of uncertainty. But, with attention to risk alone and (as always) under certain restrictive assumptions, individual preferences over risky alternatives can be represented by what is termed a von Neumann–Morgenstern utility function, u, in which the utility of a risk, or gamble, is equal to its expected

Box 6.2
Measuring risk aversion

With ordinary utility functions that are normally taken for granted, it is important to understand that these are merely representative of, or derivative from, a set of (individual) preferences for which certain properties need to be satisfied for such a utility function to exist. In addition, such utility functions, if they do exist, are only unique up to a monotonic transformation (in other words, with given indifference curves, the numbers that are put on them, as long as they are increasing in moving upwards/outwards, do not matter – something called 'ordinal'). With von Neumann–Morgenstern utility functions, the same logic applies. They also are merely representative of, or derivative from, a set of (individual) preferences for which certain properties need to be satisfied for such a utility function to exist. But in this case there are two major differences. The first is that the preferences are expressed over probabilistic bundles. The second is that for the utility of the bundle to be equal to the expected value of its separate elements, the utility function is only unique up to linear transformation, i.e. if $u(x)$ works as such a utility function so will $au(x) + b$ for any positive scalars a and b, but $u(x)^2$, for example, will not work.

This means the utility function is what is called cardinal as opposed to ordinal, but it still leaves certain problems in measuring attitudes to risk. Previously it could be said that there is more or less utility in moving from one indifference curve to another, but it could not be said how much more utility since it depends on which of the many possible different utility functions is used, each giving the same indifference curves (as would xy, for example, as opposed to x^2y^2, with utility measured in the second case as being the square of what it would be in the first, although the derived indifference and demand curves will be the same). For the von Neumann–Morgenstern utility, however, there are different ways of measuring the extent of risk aversion with these measures being the same irrespective of which of the utility function options (unique only up to linear not monotonic transformation) is chosen. The goal in measuring attitudes to risk is to assess how curved the utility function is, as can be seen from Figure 6.3 and the difference between C and D – the more curved the utility function the greater response to the risk.

One such measure of preferences over risk, what is called absolute risk aversion, is given by: $u''(x)/u'(x)$ (this remains the same if we replace u by $au + b$). With increasing absolute risk aversion, the wealthier you become the more you are liable to reduce the risks you take.

Another measure is by way of what is called relative risk aversion, given by – $xu''(x)/u'(x)$ (this also remains the same if we replace u by $au + b$). With relative risk aversion, the wealthier you become the more you are liable to decrease the proportion of wealth you hold in risky assets.

utility (see Box 6.2). For example, for incomes x_1 and x_2 with probabilities p_1 and p_2, respectively, this means that the utility of the 'gamble' is equal to $p_1u(x_1) + p_2u(x_2)$. If such utility functions are shaped as in Diagram 6.3, they represent, in sequence, risk aversion, risk preference and risk neutrality. For example, for the first of these, as indicated, the value of the gamble ranges from u_1 for $p_1 = 1$ and $p_2 = 0$, to u_2 for $p_1 = 0$ and $p_2 = 1$. But in between, the utility of certain income $p_1x_1 + p_2x_2$, at C, always lies above the expected utility, $p_1u(x_1) + p_2u(x_2)$, at D, indicating preference for certain over risky income. So the utility function represents what is termed an aversion to risk. The opposite would be true for the second diagram (risk preferring), with risk neutrality for the third.

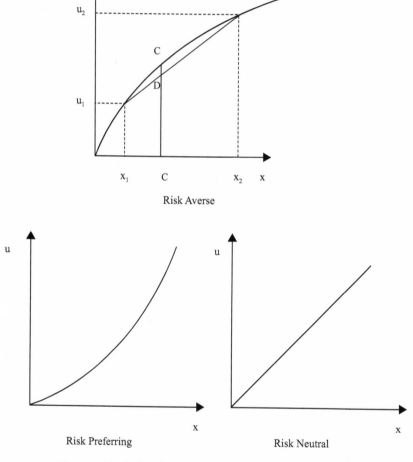

Diagram 6.3   Utility function representation of risk preferences

The value of the von Neumann–Morgenstern utility function for mainstream economics is twofold. First, it allows risk to be reduced to what is termed certainty-equivalence. It is as if a risky outcome can be replaced by a certain one in its place (lower if risk averse, etc.). Second, the approach rationalises trading in risk since this makes sense between those who are more or less risk averse relative to one another (as well as rationalising a proliferation of more or less risky trades so that there is an expansion of choice over levels and types of risk – although it is a moot point whether trading in risk redistributes it efficiently or contributes to it).

Crucially, though, the asymmetric information approach to market imperfections does not reject the conceptual reduction of uncertainty to risk but it does effectively reject the idea that risk can be treated as if certainty-equivalent. Such is evident in the idea that markets work imperfectly because of imperfect information, not perfectly if at a lower, certainty-equivalent level, and in the structures that are created between, for example, the employed and the unemployed independently of individual characteristics. Unemployment, then, is not just a lower level of certainty-equivalent, full employment.

In short, asymmetric information is a peculiarly powerful device for the mainstream in incorporating and explaining structures within markets and more broadly across economy and society. It does so, however, in a minimalist fashion, at the continuing expense of power, class and conflict, not least in labour markets where these might be thought to be particularly important.

Nonetheless, the emergence of asymmetric information in labour market theory did have one potential impact, at least in principle, namely to undermine human capital theory and its practical application. For, if there is imperfect information and (imperfect) screening in labour markets, then neither investment in, nor rewards to, human capital are secure foundations for calculating rates of return to educational investments. Such was the conclusion of one of the leading proponents of the economics of education, Mark Blaug, in the 1980s, with returns understood to be measuring screening and socialisation, for example, rather than productive skills, although these are just specific instances of the more general measurement of the deviations in reality from the assumptions necessary for the calculations. Unsurprisingly, such reservations have subsequently continued to be observed more in the breach, and the role of human capital theory in economics, and perversely across the social sciences, continues to flourish with non-economists often oblivious to the individualistic basis on which human capital is conceived even though it is applied to address issues around stratification by socio-economic variables such as class, gender and race.

6.6 Debating Minimum Wages

What has had a major impact within labour market analysis, however, is debate over the employment effects of minimum wage legislation and levels. Here, the conventional view within the mainstream is that introducing or increasing a minimum wage necessarily leads to a fall in employment on simple supply and demand analysis. Indeed, a huge majority of polled academic economists believed this alongside the equally popular nostrum surrounding the virtues of free trade. And George Stigler, the Chicago professor who is to microeconomics what Milton Friedman is to macroeconomics, essentially asserted that anyone suggesting otherwise was in breach of the first, indisputable, logical principles of economics. Unfortunately, nor did the real world have a proper understanding of these elementary principles since, in the early 1990s, David Card and Alan Krueger found that increasing the minimum wage had no negative impact on employment – the US has offered plenty of scope for empirical work as minimum wage legislation is enacted at a state level with sufficient changes to allow for before and after investigations.

First note, however, that the mainstream does allow for a positive impact on employment of minimum wage legislation in case there is a monopsony employer of labour. To show this simply, consider an extreme case where there are just two employees. One will work for a low wage, w_1, and one only for a high wage, w_2. Without a minimum wage, the firm can either employ one worker with profit, $p_1 - w$, where p is price of output and wages the only cost, or employ both with profit, $2p - 2w_2$, as each worker has to be paid the same. If p is close to w_2, then it will be more profitable to employ one worker only. But if a minimum wage is imposed above w_2, but below p, then the firm can make a bigger profit by employing both workers rather than just one as previously (although profit will be reduced considerably). More generally, the monopsony employer avoids paying higher wages by taking on fewer employees, but this is not an option with a minimum wage. There must, however, be some degree of monopoly in supplying the good, otherwise there would be entry by other firms to take advantage of the price–cost margin. More generally, if the supply-elasticity of labour relative to the wage is high enough and the demand-elasticity for the good is low enough, a minimum wage above what would be set by a firm could increase employment since the marginal cost of labour is the minimum wage (which could be below the marginal cost with a large number of employees already in place and if the wage were raised a little) and the marginal revenue will not fall that much.

To defend the position that increasing the minimum wage reduces employment such uncompetitive conditions must be put aside, but so must other considerations, as has been brought out by those who have sought to defend the orthodox position both theoretically and empirically. Thus, for example, the argument has been made that, because of increase in the minimum wage, those willing to work for that wage will be of higher quality, and so employers may be more willing to employ more of them. The increase in the minimum wage, though, is still perceived to be a source of inefficiency since those now working will have given up alternative opportunities, not least education that has become comparatively less advantageous in terms of income foregone. This, then, attaches any positive employment effects of raising the minimum wage to lifetime decisions over educational choices.

Further, it may well be that the apparent choice to work at a higher minimum wage is a spurious consequence of cyclical or secular factors – a result of what is happening to employment in any case quite independently of minimum wage legislation (think expansion in fast food outlets whose popularity, and employment, may be shifting over time independently of the minimum wage). And, possibly, there are also shifts in productivity going on that make it more favourable to demand more labour at the time that minimum wages went up.

Stepping back from these individual issues, but taking them together, it becomes apparent that in order to settle the minimum wage impact on employment debate, it is necessary to take a very broad view on how the economy is functioning as a whole. What are its growth and cyclical movements? What is happening to educational opportunities and choices and so the demographics of who might be employed? What are the competitive conditions in product and labour markets? How is the pattern of demand (for low wage goods) evolving? What is happening to productivity overall (that might shift up all wages) and in low wage sectors? And so on. Ultimately, this means that the logic of the mainstream position is that it is reduced to suggesting that if we remove all of those factors that might attach an increase in employment to an increase in the minimum wage, then we do, indeed, find that a rising minimum wage causes employment to fall.

This is little more than a tautology although, crucially, it takes a particular view of labour markets as its starting point – a simple intersection of supply and demand around which there can be considerable variation. However, this variation might be better seen, as with conditioning variables in estimating the impact of human capital, as the tail that wags the dog. Labour markets simply do not function in the way suggested by the mainstream, as is evident from the range of economic and social factors that are necessarily brought into play once confronting the minimum wage debate.

6.7 Towards Alternatives: Segmented Labour Markets

An alternative approach to labour markets takes as its starting point, not optimising individual employers and employees more or less perfectly coordinated through the market, but the historically evolved and social conditions under which labour markets are structured, and restructured, over time. An early lead in this regard was taken by what came to be known as dual labour market theory. Here is posited a double dualism. On the one hand, with the United States as exemplar, there is perceived to be a dualism between a highly monopolised, corporate industrial sector that serves core demand for mass-produced goods, and a highly competitive, small-scale sector that prospers during booms in response to higher demand but feels the pinch much more severely during recessions. By the same token, the result is to create the second, structured dualism, between secure employment at high levels of pay and with career paths and casualised, insecure jobs on low pay. In addition, there is the issue of who gets assigned to which jobs. There is the presumption that discrimination in access to the more advantageous jobs, both in getting them in the first place and proceeding to better jobs within firms for those already employed (so-called internal labour markets), reflects discrimination by race and gender, as well as the presence of more or less formally organised and closed communities in the recruitment process.

From dual labour markets, however, it is but a short step to what is termed segmented labour market theory. There is no reason why labour markets should be subject to simple dualisms on the demand side, with more complex structures of employment across industrial and other sectors (not least the role of the state as employer), and with the secondary sectors being both heterogeneous and playing a broader role than cushion for cyclical demand. A multiplicity of factors prevail on the demand side for labour, not just scale of enterprise and competitiveness, but capital intensity, sunrise or sunset sectors, technological dynamism, and so on. And, similarly, on the supply side for labour there are considerations of race, gender, location, age, unionisation, etc. Together these are deemed to mark out (segmented) labour market structures with corresponding wages and conditions, varying over hours of labour, types of work, fringe benefits, etc. Interestingly, the segmented labour market approach was in part inspired by the idea that certain segments required minimum wage protection so confined were its workers from opportunities for access to other segments with better wages and conditions, in sweated services for example.

Significantly, initially at least, the mainstream was extremely dismissive of the segmented labour market approach, considering it too empirically driven and without theory. By the latter is meant an absence of mainstream theory based on TA^2, for which the role of social structures as opposed to optimising individuals is notably absent. By the early 1990s, however, with the asymmetric information approach to labour markets in full swing, explanation for labour market structures came on to the agenda, since they were seen as compatible with agents optimising in the face of imperfect information.

What, however, the segmented labour market approach, let alone newer mainstream labour market theory, tends to overlook is what was emphasised by Marx and subsequent Marxists. This is how work, what is termed the labour process, is itself organised (a striking parallel with the black box of reducing production to choice over inputs and outputs). What exactly are the implications that flow from a situation in which what underpins the nature and development of work is the imperative of expanding profitability (something that might be seen as a major factor explaining why work is perceived as a disutility, not necessarily from the nature of work but from its intensity, duration and lack of participation in decision-making over process and product, let alone insecurity of employment itself). Nor is this simply a matter of recognising one further factor amongst those contributing to the segmenting of labour markets. Rather, work organisation, and negotiation and conflict over it, in conjunction with the other factors involved in segmenting, mean that labour markets are not only differentiated from one another, but also that each labour market segment is differentiated from others, in who gets what job, and under what conditions, and subject to different determinants and dynamics. In short, top accountants belong not only to separate but also entirely different labour markets than building labourers. The labour market for sweated, casualised work with low productivity and uncertain markets is distinct in how it functions from that for a high-tech industry, with career structures and security of employment.

A further issue in how labour markets function is how wages are determined. In contrast to the mainstream view on minimum wages, rewards to labour and levels of employment tend to increase over time alongside productivity increase. This represents a sharing of the rewards of such productivity increase between capital and labour (quite apart from taxes, financial costs, etc.). Supply and demand analysis for labour does not appear to offer an answer to how this division takes place. More important would appear to be the strength of organisation of labour, and how and whether it can raise its standards of living (whether through wage payments or otherwise, such as state provision). In other words, when and how do education and health, a motor car and central heating, become norms in settling wages. Once again, alongside factors such as levels of investment, sources of productivity increase and discrimination by race and gender, the microeconomics of labour markets can be seen to be contingent upon prior consideration of broader historical and social factors.

6.8 Further Thoughts and Readings

Much of the account offered here is covered in much greater detail in Fine (1998), with the approach to wage determination, briefly mentioned above, dovetailing with the discussion of consumption in Chapter 2 (how do norms of consumption get established and covered by wages, rather than vice versa). For an overview of the minimum wage debate, and its evolution, see Leonard (2000), Neumark and Wascher (2007) and Herr et al. (2009). For a critical discussion of the evolution of how the mainstream has understood the nature of work, see Spencer (2008). For an introduction to Marxist understandings of the labour process, see Tinel (2012). Lazonick (1981) offers a classic comparative (UK versus US) study of how the organisation of work affects choices of technology, productivity and composition of output in cotton spinning – in sharp contrast to mainstream reliance upon production functions and relative prices of capital and labour.

7
Whither Microeconomics: Upside-Down or Inside-Out?

7.1 Overview

The discipline of economics was profoundly shaken by the Global Financial Crisis, not least for having been complacent about economic prospects prior to the crisis, failing to predict it and even struggling to explain it after the event. Inevitably, the corresponding criticism focused upon the treatment of macroeconomics in general and of finance in particular. The longer-term impact upon how economics will evolve is difficult to discern at the time of writing, not least because the contest over change has turned upon the efforts of students demanding more pluralism and marginalised heterodox economists as against an established profession that primarily remains complacent about its methods and the content of its theory. Primarily, the orthodoxy's response has been to shift towards acknowledging the greater incidence of market imperfections, the greater incidence of behavioural imperfections and the greater need for more realism.

Essentially, this is a case of *plus ça change, toujours la même chose*. The contrast with the response to the crisis of the 1930s, and even of the 1970s, is striking. One witnessed the division between microeconomics and macroeconomics and the emergence of the Keynesian revolution, and the other gave rise to the monetarist counter-revolution which, arguably, set the discipline on track to the extremes to which it has now been driven. Whatever their relative merits, major changes in the discipline resulted from major economic events. The same, as yet, does not seem to be the case today.

Why is this? Hopefully, the beginnings of an answer are to be found in the text offered here. First and foremost is to recognise that, whilst the crisis has revealed the weaknesses in macroeconomics and financial economics, these are merely the tip of an iceberg of deficiencies within the discipline. Second, this is in part because both of these topics have increasingly been reduced to microeconomic considerations, or foundations. Third, these microfoundations themselves are narrowly conceived if not fundamentally flawed. As a result, fourth, it is not just macroeconomics and finance that are subject to deficient treatment but other topics too, not least distribution, technical change and so on.

These assertions need to be handled with some care. In the past, it used to be reasonable to claim that microeconomics simply overlooked the role of factors that lay outside the laws of the market reduced to individual optimising behaviour. This is no longer the case, as the discipline has found ways to bring back in more or less whatever variables it likes. But whether it does so satisfactorily, burdened as it is from its starting point in the optimising behaviour of individuals in the context of perfect outcomes from perfect competition, is questionable. Such is the thrust in Section 7.2, looking at industrial policy from the perspective of microeconomic principles.

7.2 From Microeconomics to Industrial Policy

At its core, organised around the development and consolidation of the technical apparatus and technical architecture of microeconomics (TA^2), microeconomics has been characterised in earlier chapters as having gone through a journey of implosion in upon itself, a reductionism to core methods, concepts and assumptions, governed entirely by the goals of extracting the conditions for suitably behaved supply and demand curves, at both individual and aggregate levels, not least on the basis of the narrowly conceived optimising behaviour of homo economicus. From this implosion, formally completed by the time of the formalist revolution of the 1950s, the TA^2 has paradoxically provided the basis for a Big Bang of economics imperialism across the discipline of economics itself and social sciences more generally. It has shifted the balance between its history (one part of individual economic behaviour applied purely to supply and demand upon the market) and its logic (the derivation of universal principles around utility and production functions, and optimisation, efficiency and equilibrium applied to the allocation of scarce resources between competing ends) overwhelmingly in favour of its logic, steadily if not precipitously incorporating further explanatory variables and scope of application. The result has been further tensions both between the reduced principles on which explanation is based and the scope of what is to be explained, and between those reduced principles and others that might inconsistently, even incoherently, be appended to them.

In short, the BBI via TA^2 of previously excluded considerations points to the need for a turning upside-down of the relationship between the microeconomic and the macroeconomic (meaning a systemic, holistic analysis, not the narrowly defined field of macroeconomics itself). It is necessary to take some sort of position on the nature of the economic system itself before considering how to analyse individual parts.

Such a conclusion has also been drawn from across the more detailed microeconomic material presented here. Whether for the consumer, the producer, competition, technical change or labour markets, the more the analysis is pursued within the mainstream, the more it inevitably is drawn to requiring a macro framework within which to be located. And such a conclusion also follows from issues not covered here in any detail, such as the role of institutions and the state, distribution and inequality, and, especially in the wake of the global crisis, the systemic nature of the financial system. For those doggedly, or should that be dogmatically, committed to microeconomics as such, there is always the option of reducing whatever essential part of macroanalysis that raises its inconvenient head to optimising or modified individual behaviour, allowing for endogenous preferences, strategic behaviour, etc. These in turn point to other systemic factors that need to be addressed before locating the individual.

Is it not simpler just to let go, delve back or across into the history or economic thought and heterodox economics, respectively, and begin with the macro as the precursor for specifying the micro, as has been traditional within and around the discipline of economics (and political economy) prior to the emergence and flawed triumph of mainstream microeconomics? There are plenty of such heterodox traditions with which this can be done, ranging over the social economics of Weber and Schumpeter, the evolutionary economics of Veblen, the value theories of Smith, Ricardo and Marx, and the effective demand- and finance-oriented perspectives of post-Keynesianism. And there is equally an abundance of insights to be drawn from alternative methodologies, methods, theories and conceptualisations. And each of these cuts variously across variables such as class, power and conflict that are notably absent, other than in reduced form, from the mainstream.

But there is a further lesson from working within, and towards working outside, mainstream microeconomics: this is not only that analysis within the mainstream points to the need to break with its individualistic methodology, but also that there are a multiplicity of factors underpinning the complexity of microeconomic analysis – as apparent here, especially from working through the mainstream for analysis of competition and labour markets.

This renders it even more imperative that complexity is grounded within a macro framework. Consider industrial policy, for example. A standard starting point for the mainstream is that there should be a move towards free trade by reduction in tariffs (although the theory of the second best, see Chapter 3, should sound alarm bells on this even from within the mainstream). This result, though, depends upon defining protection satisfactorily, being able to measure it sensibly (to say whether it will have gone down or not), and being able to draw the conclusion of enhanced outcomes as a result. Without going into details, literature within the mainstream suggests that to be able to do this requires a whole host of unacceptable assumptions, such as only two goods in the economy, no scale economies, perfect competition, no non-tradeables and no interaffiliate trade between multinationals (although this now makes up something like 50 per cent of trade in practice).

This exercise is, however, not entirely negative even if it totally undermines the mainstream arguments for reducing protection. For it brings to the fore that a properly constituted trade policy would need to take into account the various factors that have been so irresponsibly set aside in the rush to promote free trade. It also suggests that traditionally separate areas of policy, such as trade, technology and competition policy, should not be treated independently of one another. It also follows that the concept of comparative advantage, so prominent in (industrial) policymaking, is simply ill-founded as it seeks to ground both understanding and policymaking in a more or less deterministic account of the neutrally conceived resources that are presumed to be contained within a national economy. At best this is taken as a point of departure, as industrial policy becomes a debate over whether it is best to leave comparative advantage to the market, to support the picking of comparative advantage or, most interventionist of all, to use the state to set about creating comparative advantage. Significantly, this does not mean that mainstream microeconomics is unambiguously in favour of laissez-faire, and it has never been so given its preoccupation with market failures of various sorts. Effectively, though, comparative advantage does reduce both the nature and the goals of industrial policy to reliance upon an enhanced market without regard to broader economic and social factors. Fundamentally, mainstream industrial policy, like the microeconomics from which it derives, suffers from neglect of the formation of class interests, the exercise of power and the conflicts over these.

7.2 Further Thoughts and Readings

The cursory discussion of industrial policy offered here is merely designed to whet the appetite, indicating how mainstream microeconomic theory points to its own inadequacies as well as offering some of the factors to be covered in formulating alternatives. I have attempted to do this at length in Fine (2011c). Although, as observed throughout this text, there is no necessary connection between mainstream microeconomics and antipathy to industrial (and other forms of microeconomic) policy, this has inevitably been the direction taken over the 30 years of neoliberalism. Indeed, in the wake of the global crisis it has been loudly proclaimed that industrial policy is once more back on the agenda. However, this has been heavily oriented around piecemeal, discretionary intervention geared towards the correction of market imperfections, with the pursuit of comparative advantage in one way or another to the fore. For a critique of such perspectives, see Fine and Van Waeyenberge (2013). The most prominent holistic way of addressing industrial policy in the most recent period has been by reference to the developmental state, and the corresponding success of the East Asian Newly Industrialising Countries. However, this too has been diluted after having been taken off the agenda around the Asian crisis of 1997/8. For a critical overview of the developmental state paradigm, see Fine et al. (eds) (2012). Also prominent in industrial policy over the neoliberal period has been privatisation. For a critical review of how the mainstream has approached the topic, see Fine (1990) and Bayliss and Fine (eds) (2008).

Otherwise, and more generally (as already indicated), it is important to acknowledge that microeconomics has become endlessly inventive, not least in light of the latest phase of economics imperialism. New variables and techniques, motivations and models are forever on the agenda, although the predilection remains for a lingering attachment to the core content defined by, and reduced to, TA^2. Hopefully this text will assist those in critically appraising the new, newer and newest microeconomics as it continues to evolve and wherever it places itself – somewhere between greater claims to realism and esoteric models for their own sake.

References

Bayliss, K. and B. Fine (eds) (2008) *Whither the Privatisation Experiment?: Electricity and Water Sector Reform in Sub-Saharan Africa*, Basingstoke: Palgrave Macmillan.

Bayliss, K., B. Fine and M. Robertson (2013) 'From Financialisation to Consumption: The Systems of Provision Approach Applied to Housing and Water', Fessud Working Paper Series, no. 2, http://fessud.eu/wp-content/uploads/2013/04/FESSUD-Working-Paper-021.pdf (accessed December 2015).

Bertrand, E. (2010) 'The Three Roles of the "Coase Theorem" in Coase's Works', *European Journal of History of Economic Thought*, vol. 17, no. 4, pp. 975–1000.

Bigo, V. and I. Negru (2014) 'Mathematical Modelling in the Wake of the Crisis: A Blessing or a Curse? What Does the Economics Profession Say?', *Cambridge Journal of Economics*, vol. 38, no. 2, pp. 329–47.

Birks, S. (2015) *Rethinking Economics: From Analogies to the Real World*, Singapore: Springer. Available in earlier version at http://ssrn.com/abstract=2466830 (accessed December 2015).

Carter, S. (2011) 'C.E. Ferguson and the Neoclassical Theory of Capital: A Matter of Faith', *Review of Political Economy*, vol. 23, no. 3, pp. 339–56.

Carter, S. (2011/12) '"On the Cobb–Douglas and All That ...": The Solow–Simon Correspondence over the Aggregate Neoclassical Production Function', *Journal of Post Keynesian Economics*, vol. 34, no. 2, pp. 255–73.

Carter, S. (2012) 'C.E. Ferguson's Lost Reply to Joan Robinson on the Theory of Capital', *Journal of the History of Economic Thought*, vol. 34, no. 1, pp. 21–41.

Chang, H.-J. (2014) *Economics: The User's Guide, A Pelican Introduction*, London: Penguin.

Chick, V. and S. Dow (2001) 'Formalism, Logic and Reality: A Keynesian Analysis', *Cambridge Journal of Economics*, vol. 25, no. 6, pp. 705–21.

Cohen, A. and G. Harcourt (2003) 'Whatever Happened to the Cambridge Capital Theory Controversies?', *Journal of Economic Perspectives*, vol. 17, no. 1, pp. 199–214.

Davis, J. (2011) *Individuals and Identity in Economics*, Cambridge: Cambridge University Press.

Dow, S. (1998) 'Editorial Introduction to the Formalism in Economics Controversy', *Economic Journal*, vol. 108, no. 451, pp. 1826–8.

Felipe, J. and J. McCombie (2013) *The Aggregate Production Function and the Measurement of Technical Change: 'Not Even Wrong'*, Cheltenham: Edward Elgar.

Fine, B. (1980) *Economic Theory and Ideology*, London: Edward Arnold.

Fine, B. (1982) *Theories of the Capitalist Economy*, London: Edward Arnold.

Fine, B. (1990) 'Scaling the Commanding Heights of Public Sector Economics', *Cambridge Journal of Economics*, vol. 14, no. 2, pp. 127–42.

Fine, B. (1992) 'Total Factor Productivity versus Realism: The South African Coal Mining Industry', *South African Journal of Economics*, vol. 60, no. 3, pp. 277–92.

Fine, B. (1996) 'A Formal Note on New Theories of International Trade and Development', *Journal of International Development*, vol. 8, no. 6, pp. 805–11.

Fine, B. (1998) *Labour Market Theory: A Constructive Reassessment*, London: Routledge. Reprinted in paperback, 2010.

Fine, B. (1999) 'Competition and Market Structure Reconsidered', *Metroeconomica*, vol. 50, no. 2, pp. 194–218.

Fine, B. (2002) *The World of Consumption: The Cultural and Material Revisited*, London: Routledge.

Fine, B. (2004) 'Economics Imperialism as Kuhnian Revolution', in P. Arestis and M. Sawyer (eds), *The Rise of the Market*, Camberley: Edward Elgar.

Fine, B. (2009) 'The Economics of Identity and the Identity of Economics?', *Cambridge Journal of Economics*, vol. 33, no. 2, pp. 175–91.

Fine, B. (2011a) 'Prospecting for Political Economy', *International Journal of Management Concepts and Philosophy*, vol. 5, no. 3, pp. 204–17.

Fine, B. (2011b) 'The General Impossibility of Neoclassical Economics', *Ensayos Revista de Economía*, vol. 30, no. 1, pp. 1–22. http://econpapers.repec.org/article/erejournl/v_3 axxx_3ay_3a2011_3ai_3a1_3ap_3a1-22.htm (accessed December 2015).

Fine, B. (2011c) 'Locating the Developmental State and Industrial and Social Policy after the Crisis', UNCTAD, *The Least Developed Countries Report 2011: The Potential Role of South–South Cooperation for Inclusive and Sustainable Development*, Background Paper, no. 3, www.unctad.org/Sections/ldc_dir/docs/ldcr2011_Fine_en.pdf (accessed December 2015).

Fine, B. (2013a) 'Economics: Unfit for Purpose', *Review of Social Economy*, vol. 71, no. 3, pp. 373–89. With longer revised version as 'Economics: Unfit for Purpose: The Director's Cut', SOAS Department of Economics Working Paper Series, No. 176, 2013, www.soas.ac.uk/economics/research/workingpapers/file81476.pdf (accessed December 2015).

Fine, B. (2013b) 'Consumption Matters', *Ephemera*, vol. 13, no. 2, pp. 217–48, www.ephemerajournal.org/contribution/consumption-matters (accessed December 2015).

Fine, B. and E. Leopold (1993) *The World of Consumption*, London: Routledge.

Fine, B. and D. Milonakis (2009) *From Political Economy to Freakonomics: Method, the Social and the Historical in the Evolution of Economic Theory*, London: Routledge.

Fine, B. and A. Murfin (1984a) *Macroeconomics and Monopoly Capitalism*, Brighton: Wheatsheaf.

Fine, B. and A. Murfin (1984b) 'The Political Economy of Monopoly and Competition: A Critique of Monopoly and Stagnation Theory', *International Journal of Industrial Organisation*, vol. 2, no. 2, pp. 13346.

Fine, B. and A. Saad-Filho (2010) *Marx's 'Capital'*, 5th edition, London: Pluto (6th edition, forthcoming, 2017).

Fine, B., J. Saraswati and D. Tavasci (eds) (2012) *Beyond the Developmental State: Industrial Policy into the 21st Century*, London: Pluto.

Fine, B. and E. Van Waeyenberge (2013) 'A Paradigm Shift that Never Was: Justin Lin's New Structural Economics', *Competition and Change*, vol. 17, no. 4, pp. 355–71. With longer revised version as 'A Paradigm Shift that Never Will Be?: Justin Lin's New Structural

Economics', SOAS Department of Economics Working Paper Series, no. 179, www.soas. ac.uk/economics/research/workingpapers/file81928.pdf (accessed December 2015).

Fourcade, M., E. Ollion and Y. Algan (2015) 'The Superiority of Economists', *Journal of Economic Perspectives*, vol. 29, no. 1, pp. 89–114.

Heilbroner, R. (2000) *The Worldly Philosophers: The Lives, Times, and Ideas of the Great Economic Thinkers*, 7th edition, London: Penguin.

Herr, H., M. Kazandziska and S. Mahnkopf-Praprotnik (2009) 'The Theoretical Debate about Minimum Wages', Global Labour University, Working Paper, no. 6, www.global-labour-university.org/fileadmin/GLU_Working_Papers/GLU_WP_No.6.pdf (accessed December 2015).

Hodgson, G. (1997) 'The Fate of the Cambridge Capital Controversy', in P. Arestis, G. Palma and M. Sawyer (eds), Capital Controversy, Post-Keynesian Economics and the History of Economics: Essays in Honour of Geoff Harcourt, volume 1, London: Routledge.

Ingrao, B. and G. Israel (1990) *The Invisible Hand: Economic Equilibrium in the History of Science*, Cambridge, MA: MIT Press.

Keen, S. (2011) *Debunking Economics: The Naked Emperor Dethroned?*, revised and expanded edition, London: Zed Books.

King, J. (2012) *The Microfoundations Delusion: Metaphor and Dogma in the History of Macroeconomics*, Cheltenham: Edward Elgar.

Lawson, T. (2003) *Reorienting Economics*, London: Routledge.

Lazonick, W. (1981) 'Production Relations, Labor Productivity, and Choice of Technique: British and US Cotton Spinning', *Journal of Economic History*, vol. 41, no. 3, pp. 491–516.

Lee, F. (2009) *A History of Heterodox Economics: Challenging the Mainstream in the Twentieth Century*, London: Routledge.

Lee, F. (2013) *In Defense of Post-Keynesian and Heterodox Economics: Responses to Their Critics*, London: Routledge.

Leonard, T. (2000) 'The Very Idea of Applying Economics: The Modern Minimum-Wage Controversy and Its Antecedents', *History of Political Economy*, supplement to vol. 32, pp. 117–44.

Medema, S. (2011) 'The Coase Theorem: Lessons for the Study of the History of Economic Thought', *Journal of the History of Economic Thought*, vol. 33, no. 1, pp. 1–18.

Meramveliotakis, G. and D. Milonakis (2011) 'Surveying the Transaction Cost Foundations of New Institutional Economics: A Critical Inquiry', *Journal of Economic Issues*, vol. 44, no. 4, pp. 1045–72.

Meramveliotakis, G. and D. Milonakis (2013) 'Homo Economicus and the Economics of Property Rights: History in Reverse Order', *Review of Radical Political Economics*, vol. 45, no. 1, pp. 5–23.

Milonakis, D. and B. Fine (2009) *From Political Economy to Economics: Method, the Social and the Historical in the Evolution of Economic Theory*, London: Routledge.

Mirowski, P. (1989) *More Heat than Light: Economics as Social Physics, Physics as Nature's Economics*, Cambridge: Cambridge University Press.

Neumark, D. and Wascher, W. (2007) 'Minimum Wages and Employment', Forschungsinstitut zur Zukunft der Arbeit, Institute for the Study of Labor, Discussion

Paper Series, no. 2570, http://old.mindestlohn.de/material/studien_und_dokumente/
   trendwende/neumark_wascher_minimum_wages.pdf (accessed December 2015).

Sato, H. (2005) '"Total Factor Productivity vs. Realism" Revisited: The Case of the South
   Korean Steel Industry' *Cambridge Journal of Economics*, vol. 29, no. 4, pp. 635–55.

Spencer, D. (2008) *The Political Economy of Work*, London: Routledge.

Tinel, B. (2012) 'Labour, Labour Power and the Division of Labour' in Fine, A. Saad-Filho,
   with M. Boffo (eds), *The Elgar Companion to Marxist Economics*, Cheltenham: Edward
   Elgar.

Van Staveren, I. (2014) *Economics after the Crisis: An Introduction to Economics from a
   Pluralist and Global Perspective*, London: Routledge.

Wiener, J. (2011) 'What Begat Property?', *History of Political Economy*, vol. 43, no. 2,
   pp. 353–60.

Index

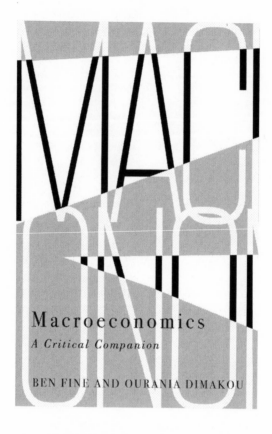